Parke Hunter Cox, Jr:
"The Smooth-Talking Industry Man"

Barbara Ann Carter Cox

Copyright © 2024 Barbara Ann Carter Cox

All rights reserved. No part of this book may be reproduced in any form or by any electronic or mechanical means, including information storage and retrieval systems, without permission in writing from the publisher, except by reviewers, who may quote brief passages in a review.

eBook ISBN: 978-1-955312-84-4

Print ISBN: 978-1-955312-77-6

Printed in the United States of America

Story Corner Publishing & Consulting, Inc.

Chesapeake, VA 23321

Storycornerpublishing@yahoo.com

www.StoryCornerPublishing.com

Table of Contents

Introduction: A Legacy of Love and Leadership

Chapter 1: Baby Hunter Born in Surry, Virginia

Chapter 2: History of Surry

Chapter 3: Hunter's Parents and Grandparents

Chapter 4: Hunter's Schools

Chapter 5: Marriage: Hunter & Barbara

Chapter 6: Residences

Chapter 7: Hunter's Golf Career

Chapter 8: Norfolk Redevelopment and Housing Authority

Chapter 9: Director of Industrial Development for the City of Chesapeake

Chapter 10: Our Trip to Europe

Chapter 11: Volvo-The Mystery Company

Chapter 12: Hunter's Retirement

Chapter 13: Sara's Interview

Chapter 14: Hunter's Legacy

Conclusion: A Life Well Lived

Acknowledgements

Dedication

I dedicate this book to everyone who crossed paths with my husband, Hunter Cox, Jr.

Introduction: A Legacy of Love and Leadership

Parke Hunter Cox, Jr. was a man who left an indelible mark on the hearts of those who knew him and the community he cherished. A family man to his core, he poured his unwavering love and devotion into his wife, Barbara, affectionately known as Bobbie, and their three children. Their smiles were his greatest joy, and their happiness, his life's mission.

As a businessman, Hunter was both visionary and compassionate. His smooth charisma and heartfelt conviction inspired others to rally behind his dreams of building a better Chesapeake, VA. He was a man of action, a builder of bridges—not just in the literal sense, but in the lives he touched and the partnerships he forged.

His brilliance shone early, excelling in academics, graduating at the top of his class, and leaving a legacy of excellence in sports. Hunter's name appeared in the daily newspaper countless times, not for controversy, but for the admirable things he accomplished. Whether on the field, in the boardroom, or among his neighbors, he exemplified integrity, discipline, and a steadfast moral compass.

Hunter's faith was his guiding light. He saw the good in everyone, choosing love over judgment, and radiating the love of God in everything he did. His presence was a gift, his absence an ache. Though his earthly journey has ended, his values and spirit live on in the family, friends, and community that he so dearly loved.

This autobiography is not merely the story of his life but a testament to the man he was and the legacy he leaves behind. Parke Hunter Cox, Jr., will forever hold a place in our hearts. He is gone but never forgotten.

With love,
Barbara (Bobbie)

Hunter Cox: The Man

Why was Hunter Cox nicknamed "The Smooth-Talking Industry Man"? With his charisma and persuasive skills, he successfully enticed 405 industries from around the world to establish operations in the United States. Among his achievements, he convinced many European companies to set up shops in Chesapeake, laying the groundwork for the city's financial future.

"Chesapeake's Altitude Position"

"The city's success in attracting industry can be attributed to the smoothest talker ever to hit the area—Hunter Cox," says G. Robert House. Known for his tact and finesse, Cox has a unique ability to connect with people, which is essential to building successful industrial sites.

Hunter Cox, Chesapeake's Industrial Director, refers to himself as a modern-day bandit—and he's proud of it. With a grin, he remarks, "They're trying to get me to set my sights on Portsmouth, but my vision is firmly here."

"Cox Brings Industry to Chesapeake"

"I like to fight," Cox admits with a grin. "Every city in the United States has someone like me competing to attract industries. It's a fierce competition."

Despite working with a modest budget, Cox relies on his longstanding connections, sharp instincts, and relentless determination—a winning formula that has reaped rewards for Chesapeake. New industries bring lower property taxes, enhanced municipal services, and more jobs for the community.

A Salute to Parke Hunter Cox, Jr.

Hunter Cox has been called many things: the savior of the city, an egotistical tyrant, a salesman, a smooth talker, and even the director of industrial clients searching for a new home. Love him or loathe him, everyone in business, government, or politics knows his name.

Cox is unapologetically proud of his reputation. "I've made a lot of good friends and a lot of good enemies," he says in his signature Southern drawl. "And I'm just as proud of the latter as I am of the former. A man is known by his friends *and* his enemies."

While some may criticize his methods, few can argue with his results. "Everyone might not agree with the way I do things," Cox says, "but I get results." Under his leadership, Chesapeake has earned its place on the industrial map—a map every aspiring city wants to be on.

"Other cities have slick promotional packages showcasing their industrial advantages," says one industrialist. "The only slick package Chesapeake has is Hunter Cox."

Hunter's Bold Moves

Cox's aggressive pursuit of new opportunities sometimes ruffles feathers. One of his most ambitious targets? The U.S. Navy's 489-acre St. Juliens Creek Ammunition Depot in Chesapeake. Cox was so determined to repurpose the property for private industry that the Navy banned him from the base. Unfazed, Cox resorted to aerial reconnaissance to gather the information he needed.

"It's perfect for industrial users who need deep-water access," Cox says of the facility, which he believes is currently underutilized.

Facing Criticism with Confidence

Critics often question Cox's methods, but he meets them with a smile and a shrug, daring them to take their best shot. His approach to industrial recruitment is highly confidential, as industries demand discretion during negotiations.

"Imagine if employees of a company heard their jobs were relocating to Chesapeake before a decision was finalized," Cox explains. "The damage could be irreversible, even if the company ultimately decided not to move."

Cox's Impact on Chesapeake

Ed Cooke, a sales expert at Greenbriar Industrial Park, admires Cox's self-reliance. "Hunter is his own man," Cooke says. "He keeps a low profile and doesn't ask for help. Some might prefer a more visible approach, but I think he's highly competent."

Gilbert Westerhof, corporate vice president of Netherlands-based Koppens Automatic, agrees. His company chose Chesapeake's Industrial Park over other locations because of Cox.

"Hunter Cox is the reason we're here," Westerhof says. "He looks you straight in the eye and tells it like it is. He makes no empty promises but offers his full support. We'd hire him away from the city in a heartbeat if we could."

Indeed, the only "slick package" Chesapeake needs is Hunter Cox himself.

P. Hunter Cox

THE MAN

PARKE HUNTER COX, JR.

The Myth

I. P. Cash (I Pay Cash)

The Legend

Hunter

Head of Industrial Development (Chesapeake, VA)

Hunter Cox

May 1936-Feburary 2022

Cox-Carter Family History Trivial Pursuit Game
Designed by Barbara Ann Carter Cox

Description:

- Top left: Cox residence (331 East McGinnis Circle, Norfolk, VA)
- Top Right: Cox residence (4343 Bruce Rd, Chesapeake, VA)

- Bottom left: "The Pond" Claremont family gathering place for boating and fishing.
- Bottom Right: Cocks Cox Coat of Arms.

- Cox "Shell" signifies Paul and his collection of shells.

- Salt and Pepper painting signifies Barbara's collection of shakers.
- Painting of shoes signifies Suzanne Cox's collection of shoes.
- 2nd row with Blue Buck Soda Bottle signifies Hunter's bottle collection.
- 3rd row "Lone Stamp" signifies Parke's collection of stamps.

Cox Code of Arms

The Cox Name

COCK(E), COX — There were three Old English words, two of them spelled cocc and one spelled coc, which could have formed this name. It is now impossible to differentiate among them.

One cocc meant a male bird, especially one that strutted. This word became a common nickname for a pert boy and later was used for dishwashers, apprentices and servants. Two references indicated that the name might have been applied to an overseer or watchman in the sense of "boss." It also was used as a given name.

The other cocc meant "heap, hillock." A heap of grass was a "haycock," a heap of sand or rock was a "hillcock," now "hillock."

The coc, pronounced "coke," meant a cook. A Welsh and Cornish word, coch, meaning "red," could have formed some of these early names. The German name Koch, meaning "cook," could have been Americanized into Cox or Cock instead of Cook.

Burke's General Armory lists 59 arms for the six spellings.

In Virginia, the following are only a few of the various spellings of people who held early land grants. William Coxe arrived in Elizabeth City County in 1610 and William Cox held 100 acres there in 1628. Hugh Cox held 500 acres in Charles City County in 1635. A William Cox held 150 acres in Henrico County in 1636. Lewis Cocke held land in Warwick County prior to 1635. Richard Cocke, "Gent," held 3,000 acres in Henrico County in 1636.

Parke Hunter Cox Jr.

Married

Barbara Ann Carter

September 29, 1957

Parke Hunter Cox, III, born July 8, 1959

Suzanne Cox, born October 5, 1961

Paul Carter Cox, born June 9, 1964

Suzanne Cox married Ronald Craig Martin June 10, 1991

- Jaclyn Martin born February 28, 1992

Parke Hunter Cox, III married Lisa Ann Bowker February 27, 1993

- Allison Martin born April 6, 1993
- Carter Cox Martin born July 13, 1995
- Parke Hunter Cox IV, born April 2, 1996

Paul Carter Cox married Suzanne Lea Schomberg June 29, 1996

- Sara Ealise Cox born January 28, 2005

- Anna Elizabeth Cox born July 2, 2008

Suzanne Cox married Joseph Walter Stickle, Jr. December 31, 2015

Carter Cox Martin married Katherine Kimiko Arita June 3, 2017

The Cox tree continues to grow and there are more members of the Cox family to this date.

"The apple does not fall far from the tree"

This scroll was designed and hand-stitched by Barbara Ann Carter Cox

Chapter 1:
Baby Hunter Born in Surry, Virginia

Parke Hunter Cox, Jr. "Hunter" was born May 7, 1936, in Richmond, Virginia. He was the son of Parke Hunter Cox, Sr. "Buster" and Hazel Davies Turner Cox, and the grandson of Paul Clifford Cox and Maude Evelyn Gilliam Cox, known as "Big Mama."

Hunter in Surry, 12024 Rolfe Highway at Christmas

Silhouette of Hunter

Baby Hunter

Chapter 2:
History of Surry

Hunter was born on May 7, 1936, in Richmond, Virginia, and spent his childhood in Surry County, residing at 12024 Rolfe Highway. Surry County is located in the heart of Virginia, often referred to as "The Cradle of the Republic," nestled just across the "Lordly James River."

This historic area holds the distinction of being one of the earliest points of English colonization in America. On May 5, 1609, English settlers landed near what is now the town of Claremont before tying their ships to the trees at Jamestown on May 13, 1609.

Surry County was officially formed in 1652 from the original shires of James City. It first gained representation in the House of Burgesses on November 25, 1609, with William Thomas, William Edwards, and George Stevens serving as its inaugural representatives.

The James River

---

1. Marriages of Surry County 1768 - 1825 (Preface by Catherine L. Knorr)
2. A.W. Bohannon

Surry is one of seventeen Virginia counties named after English shires, though spelled without the "e" as it is in England. The county is rich in history, home to many notable landmarks. Among them are the Surry Courthouse, Smithfield Fort Plantation, and the Rolfe Property, which was part of the land given by Chief Powhatan to John Rolfe and Pocahontas as a wedding gift. Additionally, there is Arthur Allen's home, built around 1660, which is now known as Bacon's Castle after it was seized and occupied by Nathaniel Bacon and his men in 1676.

Map of Seventeen Virginia Counties

---

1. Catherine Lindsay Knorr)
2. Standard's Colonial Register

For some time, Surry was considered part of Jamestown, as many colonists in Jamestown had plantations "across the water." Today, Surry is a lovely rolling, half cultivated, half wooded area. Three hundred years ago, it must have been a veritable paradise.

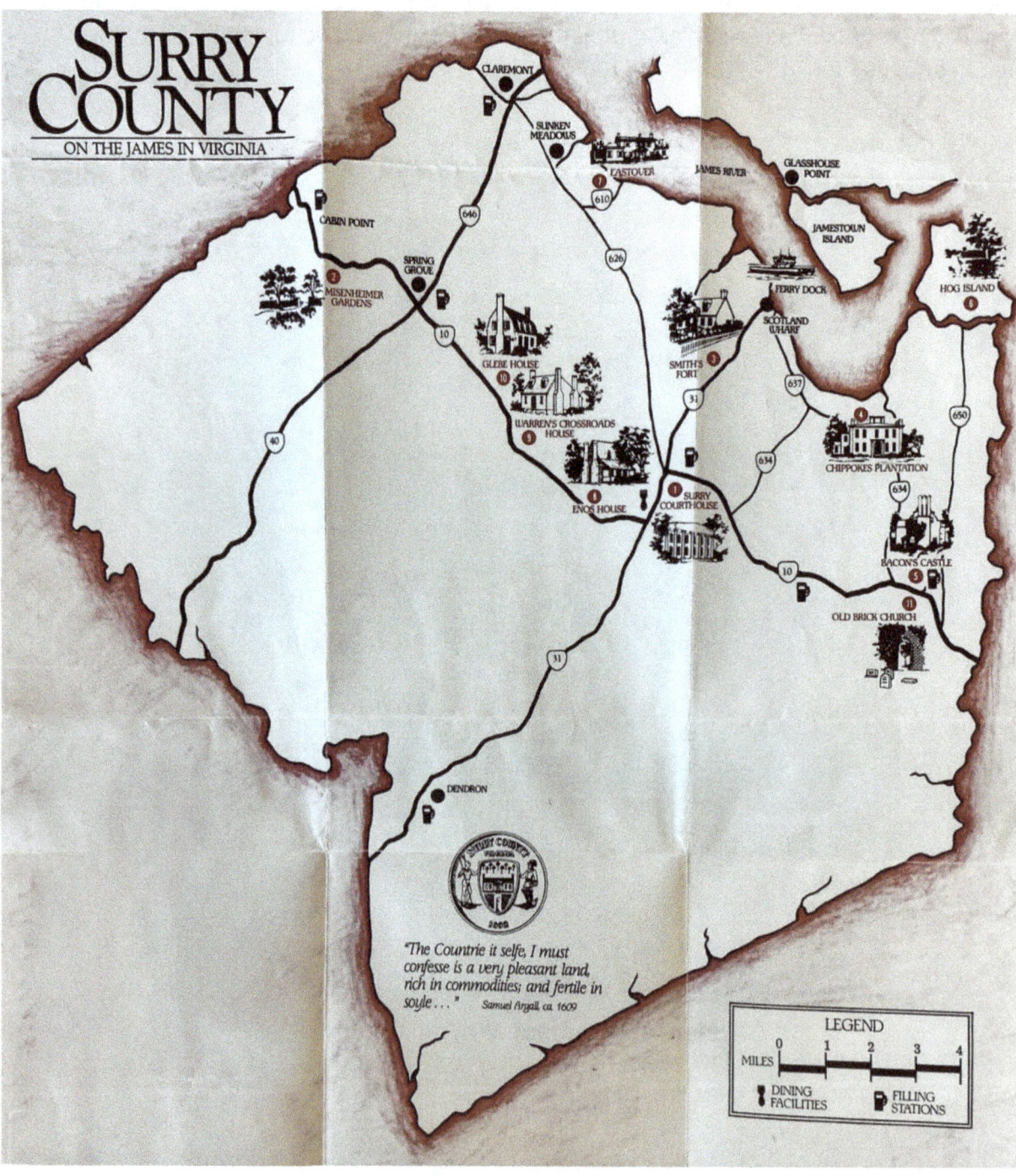

Surry Courthouse

English colonists first arrived in Surry County on May 5, 1607. Captain George Percy wrote of Surry's fine paths through the woods, its pleasant springs, and "the goodliest corn fields that I have seen in any country." Originally part of James City County, Surry became a separate county in 1652. The county, long and narrow, ran northeast to southwest and was divided by the Blackwater River, which later became the boundary between Surry and Sussex counties.

By 1700, the land north of the Blackwater River was well settled, but the area south of the river was not legally open for settlement until 1710.

The Surry Monument, located at the Surry Courthouse, was erected on August 2, 1910, in memory of Confederate soldiers. Although the monument is no longer standing as of 2024, it remains a significant part of the county's history.

The Surry County Courthouse, located at the intersection of "McIntosh's Corner" on Route 10, is at least the sixth courthouse in the county's history. The previous courthouse, a classical structure, was destroyed by fire in 1906. It was rebuilt with a two-story Roman portico, only to be burned again in 1922.

Surry County Courthouse

---

1. Hennings Statues Vol. IV pg. 546

Big Mama's letter concerning Surry Courthouse:

"The courthouse burned down January 12th, 1922. The prisoners in jail woke me up a few minutes past 1:00 A.M.; I then woke Paul and the boys. The blaze was then bursting through the top of the roof. Mr. Bohannon, Surry's historian, offered $150 to anyone who would go in the building to get his books. Finally, he went in because no one took the offer. He cut his wrist on the window glass as he entered. Right before Mr. Bohannon got out of the building, the fire entered the room where he was.

Of course, Paul Cox was interested to know who started the fire, so he found tracks leaving the place, and when it got light, he, Mr. Sadler, Mr. Berryman, and Mr. Spratley tracked them to their homes. They caught one and Paul and Mr. Hester hunted for the others. Paul and the men didn't get back home until 2:00 P.M. that night."

-Big Mama.

Surry's Stories

Letter from Big Mama on June 11, 1922:

To Bernice:

"Things just happen, in every case, however, there are exceptions to the general rule. The now law-abiding sheriff of our county got "boozy" the other day and alarmed the neighborhood that night. Your daddy, P.C.C. and several others went down to see Lady Zoa, the sheriff's girlfriend, to see if she was getting the best of him. They found Zoa, calm and placid as usual. Upon being dismissed by Zoa, the men returned to their respective homes, leaving the drunken sheriff locked in the outhouse.

That's Surry for you.

Surry Auto Ford Company

The Cox family owned the Surry Auto Ford Company, located next door to Big Mama's house at 276 Church Street, Surry, VA. On June 22, 1922, a fire at the shop severely impacted the family business, forcing the closure of the location. However, the Cox family remained resilient and continued to pursue success, undeterred by the setback.

Surry Auto Ford Company

High School Yearbook Ford Ad

Chapter 3:
Hunter's Parents and Grandparents

Hunter and his mother, Hazel Davies Turner Cox

Hunter and his father, Parke Hunter Cox, Sr.

Hunter's paternal grandparents, Paul Clifford Cox and "Big Mama," lived at 276 Church Street, directly across from the Surry Courthouse. His mother, Hazel Davies Turner Cox, was a truly lovely woman. In 1952, she proudly served as Miss Liberty in a parade in Surry.

Hunter's maternal grandparents were Kilby Seth Turner and Mary Edna Gresham Turner, who played an important role in shaping the family's rich heritage.

Hunter's mama & daddy, Hazel Davies Turner Cox and Parke Hunter Cox, Sr. "Buster"

Hunter with his father, Parke Hunter Cox, Sr. and his grandfather, Kilby Seth Turner

Kilby Seth Turner worked as an engineer for the Chesapeake and Ohio Railroad. He operated the "Excursion Train," a special extension that carried South Siders from Richmond to Buckroe Beach during the 1920s and 1930s. On summer Tuesdays, the train transported church groups for a day of fun at the beach.

In our hallway, we have a painting of Kilby Seth Turner standing proudly in front of the Chesapeake and Ohio train. The artwork was created by Casey Holtzinger, a close friend of Hunter's, making it a cherished piece of our family's history.

Kilby in front of C&O Train

In 1948, engineer Kilby Seth Turner was honored with his 50-year service pin and featured in a Chesapeake and Ohio Railroad pamphlet. To celebrate the occasion, he attended a luncheon at the Mosque in Richmond, accompanied by his daughters, Mrs. Davies Turner Cox ("Sue") and Mrs. Helen Turner Crosby. Kilby Seth Turner's legacy is further commemorated by his watch fob engraved with "BL of E" (Brotherhood of Locomotive Engineers), symbolizing his dedication to the profession.

Luncheon at the Mosque in Richmond, VA

Seated:

- Paul Clifford Cox (Hunter's grandfather)
- Hunter
- Maude "Big Mama" (Hunter's grandmother)

Standing:

- Parke Hunter Cox, Sr. (Hunter's father)
- Hazel Davies Turner Cox (Hunter's mother)
- Roger Cox
- Salinda Gilliam
- Bernice Cox Willard
- Earl Fred Willard

Before Maude married Paul Clifford Cox, she lived in Petersburg at 226 Franklin Street. This was the home of the Gilliam family. When Paul and Maude were first married, they had a store in Gray, Virginia.

Paul Clifford Cox

This article was published in the *Surry Herald and Sussex* and *Surry Dispatch* on February 19, 1947, following the passing of Paul Clifford Cox, Hunter's grandfather:

"The Board of Supervisors of Surry County honors Paul Clifford Cox and, at his passing, expresses feelings of regret and sorrow. We acknowledge the intelligent and faithful services rendered by Mr. Cox. He was a man of remarkable enterprise and executive ability, and his patriotism to his county and its people was unwavering. He will be deeply missed."

Maude Evelyn Gilliam Cox "Big Mama"

Mrs. Maude Gilliam Cox, Hunter's grandmother, passed away at her home in Surry, Virginia, on April 25, 1971, at the age of 89. She was the widow of Paul C. Cox and a devoted member of Surry Baptist Church.

Funeral services were held on Tuesday at 11:00 a.m. at Blandford Cemetery in Petersburg, VA. In lieu of flowers, memorial contributions may be made to the Surry Rescue Squad or the Surry Volunteer Fire Department.

Bernice Cox Willard

Bernice Cox Willard, the daughter of Maude Evelyn Cox and Paul Clifford Cox, was Hunter's beloved aunt. She attended Averett College in 1922 and later married Fred Earl Willard of Floyd, Virginia, in 1936. Their wedding took place at "Big Mama's" house in Surry, Virginia. Bernice Cox Willard passed away in June 1980, leaving behind cherished memories of a life well lived.

Davies T. Cox

Daily Press

Tuesday, Oct. 7, 1997

Davies T. Cox
SURRY

Davies Turner Cox died Monday, Oct. 6, 1997, in Richmond. Mrs. Cox was born in Richmond and was the daughter of Kilby Seth Turner and Edna Gresham Turner. She was a member of St. Paul's Episcopal Church, Surry, and had served as a former president of the Women of the Church. She had also served as treasurer of the Episcopal Churchwomen of the Diocese of Southern Virginia. She was a former member and first president of the Woman's Club of Surry. She was a lifetime member of the Thomas Rolfe Branch, Association for the Preservation of Virginia Antiquities, and had served as its treasurer. She was the widow of Parke "Buster" Hunter Cox Sr.

She is survived by a son, Parke Hunter Cox Jr. of Chesapeake; three grandchildren, Parke Hunter Cox III of Richmond, Suzanne Cox Martin of Davidsonville, Md., and Paul Carter Cox of King George; and four great-grandchildren.

Graveside services will be held in Blandford Cemetery, Petersburg, on Wednesday, Oct. 8, at 11 a.m. by the Rev. M.O. Young.

Memorial donations may be made to St. Paul's Episcopal Church or to Surry Volunteer Rescue Squad.

Purviance Funeral Home, Wakefield, is handling arrangements.

PURVIANCE MONUMENT COMPANY
WAKEFIELD, VIRGINIA

Chapter 4:
Hunter's Schools

- Elementary School in Surry
- Surry County High School
- Augusta Military Academy (AMA)
- Hampden-Sydney College

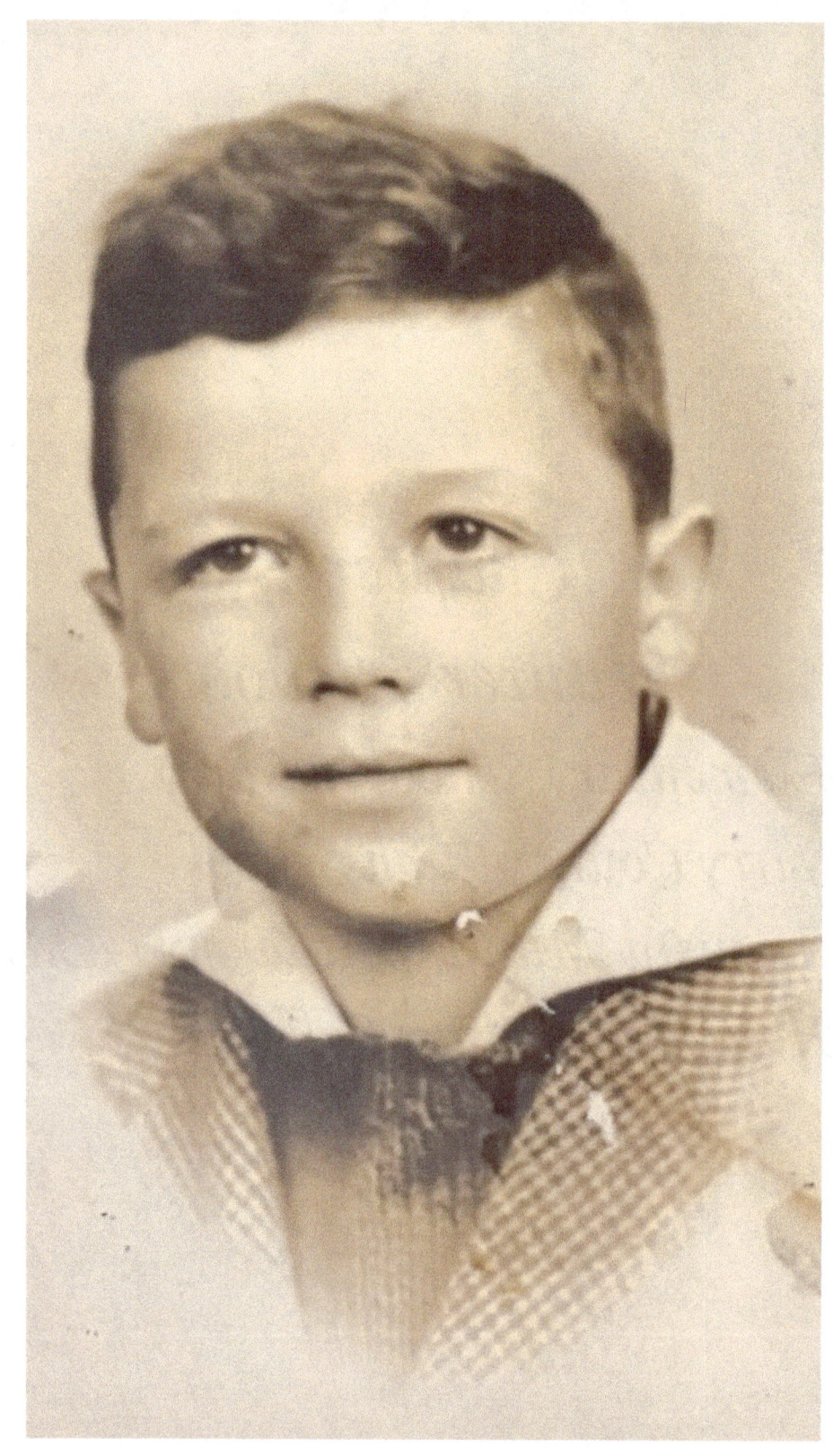

Hunter in elementary school in Surry

Baseball

Hunter was the mascot of a semipro baseball team in Surry, Va

Surry County High School

Hunter Cox

Class of 1952

Hunter was very active in high school, participating in the baseball and basketball teams and serving as an officer of the Student Council Association (S.C.A.). He attended Surry public schools during his early years, but his parents felt that he wasn't receiving the level of education he deserved. As a result, when Hunter was a junior in high school, they decided to send him to Augusta Military Academy in Virginia.

Robert Cooke, Reuben Haff, Kenneth Samuel, Edwin McGuriman, Kenneth Cofer, Hunter Cox, Eddie Epps, Bobby Lane, Malcolm Humphries, Garland Seward.

FIRST ROW: Robert Cooke, Eddie Epps, Kenneth Samuel, Hunter Cox, Bobby Lane.
SECOND ROW: David Hux, Garland Seward, Kenneth Cofer.

OFFICERS
FIRST ROW: Barbara Faison, Kenneth Samuel, Barbara Grubbs. SECOND ROW: Hunter Cox, Mrs. Rollings, Karl Haff.

S.C.A

Hunter's Senior Pictures

Hunter's high school belt buckle

40

Augusta Military Academy (AMA)

Class of 1954

Parke Hunter Cox Jr., affectionately known as "Hunt," arrived at Augusta Military Academy with a distinguished presence that exceeded the hopes of those invested in his future. Hunter quickly became a standout, earning recognition as a star in football, basketball, and baseball. He was frequently praised in the Mess Hall announcements, notably being singled out as an exceptional guard among his peers.

In addition to his athletic achievements, Hunter earned a place on the Honor Roll with distinction, balancing his rigorous academic responsibilities with his commitment to sports. His impeccable posture and military precision also added a notable presence to the Roller Rifles on parade, further showcasing his dedication and discipline during his time at AMA.

Cadet 1st Sergeant Parke Hunter Cox

Activities of 1953-54 School Year

- 86% grade average with no demerits
- "Company A" graduating senior

Teams:

- **Varsity Football end player (#76)**
- **Varsity Basketball**

14 games played

90 field goals made

87 of 140 free throws made (62%)

267 total points scored

- **Baseball**
- **Roller Rifles precision drill team**

Social & Extracurricular activities:

- May 7, 1954: accompanies First Princess Nancy Day at the 11th annual Pin-Up Dance
- Bayonet student newspaper: sports editor

Recognition:

- Best Athlete
- Best Non-Commissioned Officer
- Most Athletically Minded

- Nicknames: Hunt and Dug

Honor organization:

- Ad Astra per Aspera

***Class Prophecy:** In 1959, "Hunter Cox will have a chain of Ford Agencies under different names throughout the Southern States. He will also play some professional baseball when time permits with the New York Yankees."*

 **Hunter at AMA**

 **AMA Ribbons & Rank**

 **Best Cadet Trophy**

Commencement Programs

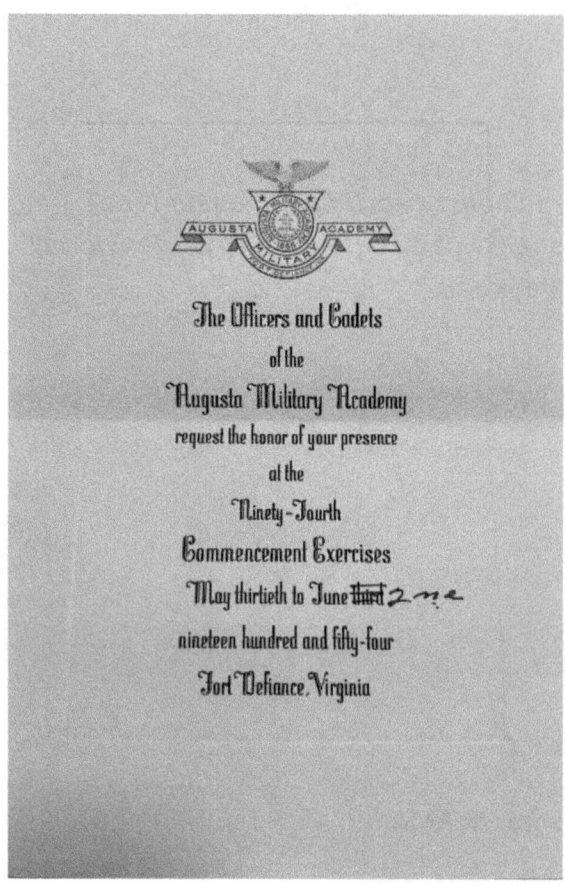

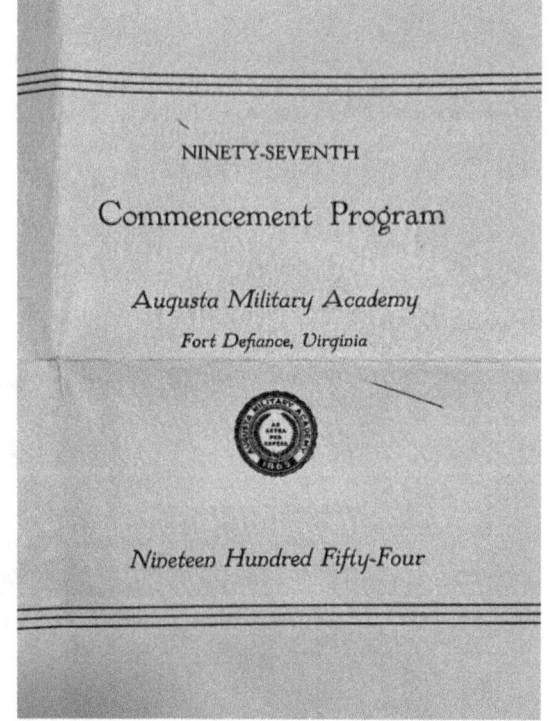

SATURDAY, MAY 29th

- 3:00 P. M.   Exhibition Drill "Roller Rifles"
- 5:30 P. M.   Dress Parade
- 7:30 P. M.   Moving Pictures
- 9:00 P. M.   Practice for Final Ball

SUNDAY, MAY 30th

- 11:30 A. M.   Baccalaureate Sermon — Old Stone Church
  Rev. James Sprunt, D.D., First Presbyterian
  Church of Raleigh, N. C.
- 4:00 P. M.   Exhibition Drill by "Roller Rifles"
- 4:30 P. M.   Full Dress Parade
- 5:20 P. M.   Sacred Concert by the Band in the Circle
- 6:30 P. M.   Reception and Buffet Supper at White Hall
- 8:00 P. M.   Final Meeting of Y. M. C. A. — Assembly Hall

MONDAY, MAY 31st

- 10:00 A. M.   Guard Mount by Junior Company
- 11:00 A. M.   Lacrosse Game
- 2:00 P. M.   Competitive Drill for Platoon Cup by all Companies
- 4:30 P. M.   Sponsor's Parade
- 8:00 P. M.   Final Celebration of Senior & Junior Ciceronian Literary Societies

TUESDAY, JUNE 1st

- 10:00 A. M.   Guard Mount by some Company
- 11:00 A. M.   Exhibition Drill by "Roller Rifles"
- 2:00 P. M.   Company Drill among all Companies for the Cup, followed by Individual Competitive Drill
- 4:30 P. M.   Graduation Parade
- 9:30 P. M.   Final Ball, Memorial Gymnasium
  Co-Presidents 1st Cadet Captain Parker Ward
  and Cadet Captain Pete Stone

WEDNESDAY, JUNE 2nd

- 10:00 A. M.   Closing Exercises — Memorial Gymnasium
  Awarding of Certificates and Diplomas, Prizes, Medals
  and Military Honors — Colonel Chas. S. Roller, Jr.
  Address to Graduating Class — Lieutenant General Edward
  H. Brooks, U. S. Army Retired
  Valedictorian — Captain Parker L. Ward, Huntington, W. Va.
- 12:15 P. M.   Delivery of Rahily Rhodes plaque by his Class Mates
  Auld Lang Syne Parade — Front of Barracks

MONDAY, MAY 31st

- 8:00 P. M.   Academic Hall
  Final Celebration of the Ciceronian Literary Societies

OFFICERS JUNIOR SOCIETY

President — Sergeant Tyrone F. Tomasek .... Maryland
Vice President — Sergeant J. Hugh Harmon .... Delaware
Secretary — Corporal Arnaldo Garcia .... Cuba
Treasurer — Corporal Larry E. Long .... Pennsylvania
Sergeant-at-Arms — Private Roger M. Quimby .... Pennsylvania

JUNIOR DECLAIMERS

Private Daniel L. Manies .... Pennsylvania
Private Marker E. Lovell .... Virginia
Private Frederick S. Womer .... Virginia
Private Terence H. Collins .... Maryland
Private Roger M. Quimby .... Pennsylvania
Sergeant J. Hugh Harmon .... Delaware

OFFICERS OF SENIOR SOCIETY

President — Captain Tomme T. Gamewell .... North Carolina
Vice President — First Lieutenant F. Edmund Burke ...... Virginia
Secretary — Private Richard A. Bramwell .... Ohio
Treasurer — Captain John C. L. Fitts .... Virginia
Sergeant-at-Arms — Captain Walter L. Stone ...... District of Columbia

SENIOR DECLAIMERS

Captain Frank C. Suter .... Virginia
Sgt. 1st Class Thomas P. Lassell .... Virginia
Second Lieutenant Bernard Y. Cockrell .... Virginia
First Sergeant Stephen F. Tomasek .... Maryland
Sgt. 1st Class Douglas Benedict .... New York
Private Stephen D. Askin .... Maryland

DEBATERS

Subject: Resolved that the President of the United States should be elected by the direct vote of the people.

AFFIRMATIVE

Second Lieutenant Manley P. Caldwell .... Florida
Sergeant Patrick E. Stanton .... West Virginia

NEGATIVE

First Sergeant Gilbert Goldstein .... Honduras
Sergeant Major Michael L. Bottino .... Virginia

CANDIDATES FOR A. M. A. DIPLOMAS 1954

Alvarez, Ricardo San Pedro .... Cuba	Gamewell, Tomme T. ..... North Carolina
Bell, John T. .... Philippine Islands	Goldstein, Gilbert .... Honduras
Bottino, Michael L. .... Virginia	Ireland, John R. Jr. ..... North Carolina
Caldwell, Manley P. .... Florida	Meals, Robert W. Jr. .... Illinois
Cox, P. Hunter J. .... Virginia	Stone, Walter L. ... District of Columbia
Dulin, Edward T. ... District of Columbia	Townsend, William G. .... Virginia
Fitts, John C. L. .... Virginia	Ward, Parker L. .... West Virginia
	Wirkus, Faustin E. .... Maryland

CANDIDATES FOR SCIENTIFIC DIPLOMAS AND HIGH SCHOOL CERTIFICATES 1954

Austin, Anthony K. .... Michigan	Keitges, James P. .... Canada
Bramwell, Richard A. .... Ohio	Kirtz, J. Phillip .... Virginia
Burnett, William L. .... Virginia	Lassell, Thomas P. .... Virginia
Cockrell, Bernard Y. .... Virginia	Phillips, Lee V. .... North Carolina
Eagles, Joseph E. Jr. .... North Carolina	Phillips, Robert I. .... Ohio
Fletcher, David E. Jr. ... West Virginia	Ray, A. Chambers, Jr. .... Virginia
Gontrum, Louis R. .... Virginia	Robertson, L. Harold .... Virginia
Griggs, T. Thomas .... Virginia	Stanton, Patrick E. ..... West Virginia
Hernandez, Francisco A. ..... New York	Suter, Franc C. .... Virginia
Hoke, Kenneth A. .. District of Columbia	Trible, George M. III .... Virginia
Jones, Jack D. .... North Carolina	Wallace, Thomas C. IV .... Virginia
	Weant, Robert W. ...... North Carolina

Hampden Sydney College

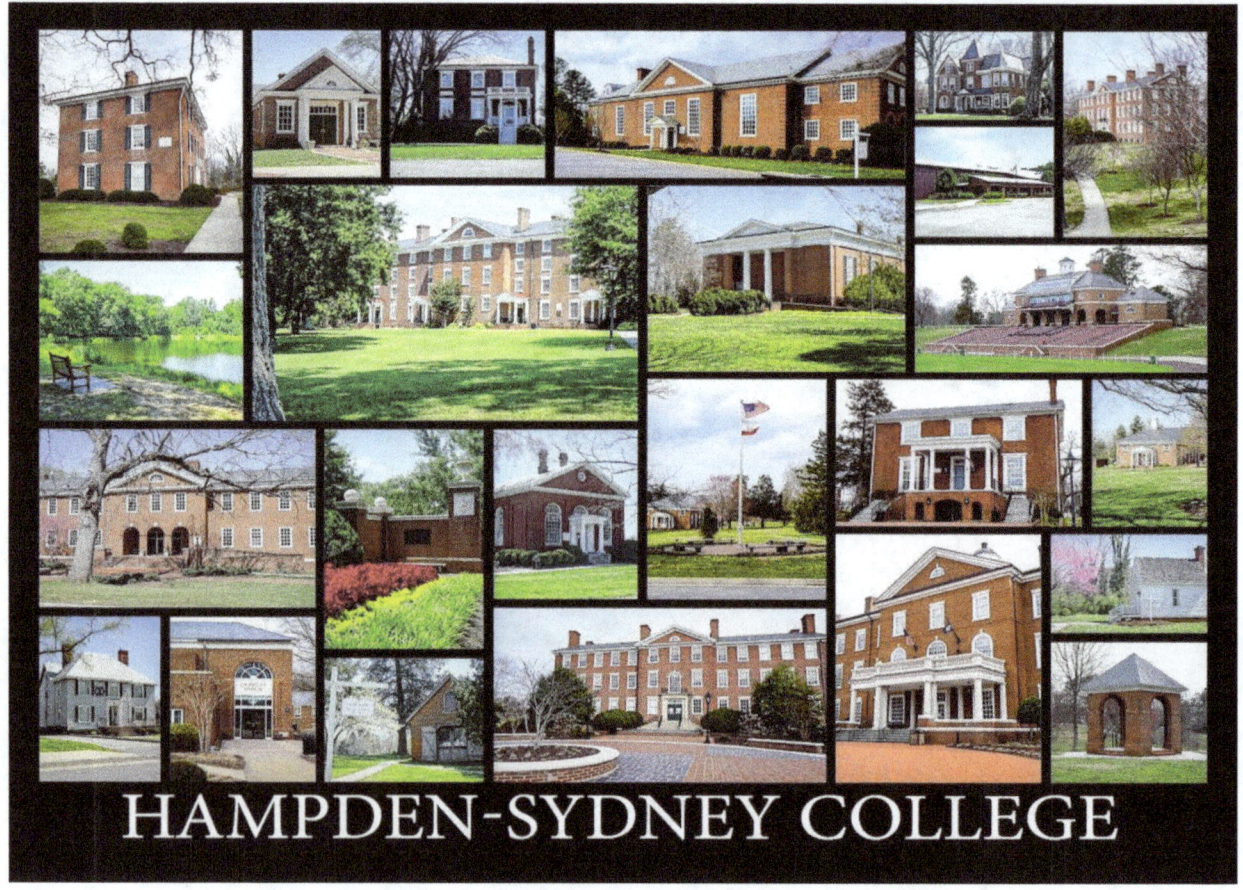

Tigers at Death Valley

Why were the athletic fields at "Hampden Sydney called "Death Valley?"

Coach Stokeley Fulton who was HSC's coach for 18 years explained that no one really knew how the fields received its name and that they were named long before he arrived in 1950. Hampden- Sydney, seven miles from Farmville played its first football team 1892 in "Death Valley."

"Death Valley" Tradition

Tradition has it that during World War I, Yankee College teams used to go down to play Hampden-Sydney's tigers. They would arrive in Farmville and were taken to Hampden-Sydney by horse and wagon. The invading teams were so frequently defeated that they started calling the field, which was situated in a valley, making for a natural amphitheater,

"Death Valley." Coach Fulton is a legend at HSC. He says, "I love coaching at Hampton-Sydney, "The Boys to Coach are the kind you want your sons to be."

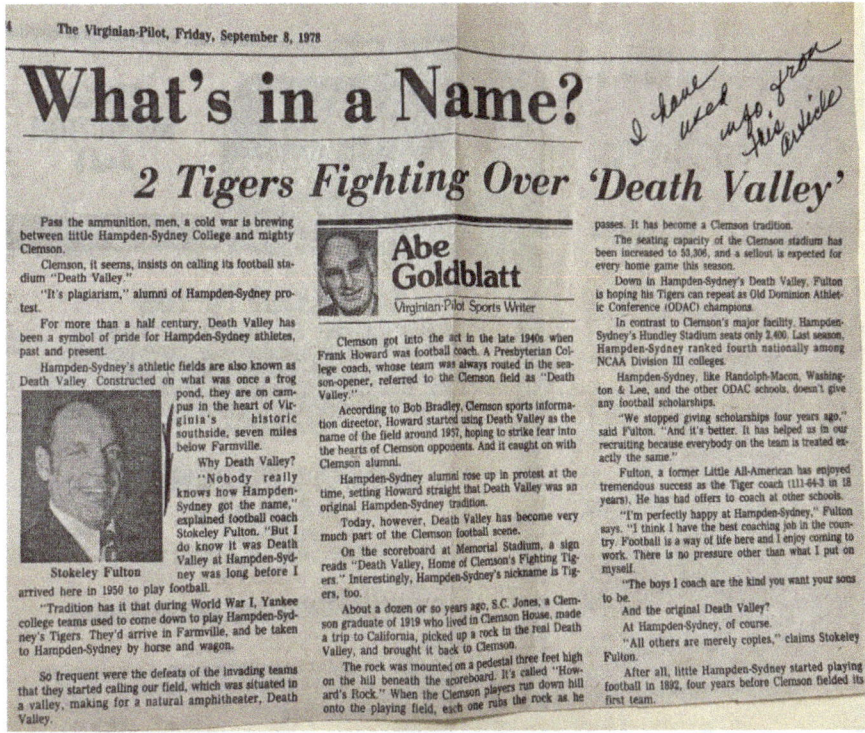

May 16, 1958

Hampden-Sydney's tigers won their first Mason-Dixon Championship by drowning Washington College 6-3 and 5-3 in title playoffs. Hunter Cox, 1st baseman, made a solo homer to help win the playoffs.

Summer 1960

Hunter played 1st baseman in the Norfolk City League at Lakewood for team L.T. Zoby, The Plumbers.

L.T. Zoby won many victories over:

The Hampton Royals

The Colonial Chevrolet

The Portsmouth Phillies

The All-Star game was July 6, 1960. In Norfolk newspapers: The L.T. Zoby gave the tight City League pennant race a "squeeze" Sunday by thrashing WGH 12-2 at Lakewood. The plumbers moved within one-half game of first place. The following City League game, L.T Zoby won!

Hunter Cox, 1st Basemen at HSC

Chapter 5:
Marriage: Hunter & Barbara

In 1955, while attending Longwood College, I met Hunter on a blind date. When he told me he was from Surry, I asked, "What? Surry, England?" Hunter laughed and replied, "No, I'm from Surry, Virginia." I admitted I had never heard of the place and had no idea where it was. Without hesitation, Hunter promised to take me there the following weekend for our second date—and he did.

That weekend was magical. We had a wonderful time and fell in love at first sight. Hunter, standing tall at 6 feet 3 inches, with black curly hair, beautiful brown eyes, a fantastic smile, and irresistible charm, swept me off my feet. He became the love of my life, and the rest, as they say, is history.

Chapter 6:
Residences

- 6416 Merle Ave. Apt C, Norfolk, Virginia was our first apartment. We had it furnished with a bed, sofa, table and two chairs.

- Our second apartment was 1228 Norview Ave., Norfolk, VA.

- Our first house was 331 East McGinnis Circle, Norfolk, VA, and our children were born there.

    - Parke Hunter Cox III was born July 8, 1959.
    - Suzanne Cox was born October 5, 1961.
    - Paul Carter Cox was born June 9,1964.

331 East McGinnis Circle, Norfolk, VA

Hunter & his daddy, "Buster" Cox on May 1966 at our home, 331 East McGinnis Circle Norfolk, Va.

When Hunter became the Director of Industrial Development in 1971, we built a house at 4343 Bruce Rd. Chesapeake, VA.

Finishing touches of our home

Our home during the holidays

Painting of our home

Chapter 7:
Hunter's Golf Career

May 23, 1963

Hole-in-one by Hunter Cox of Stumpy Lake highlighted. Cox, president of the Stumpy Lake Golf Association. Picked the tough 220-yard 17th hole for his first ace. His line drive 4-wood shot hit on the front edge of the green and rolled in during the Virginia Beach tournament.

October 9, 1967

Hunter shot a 78-7-71 to win the monthly, President's Cup Award in Tidewater Gold Association play at Lake Wright Golf Course.

May 27, 1968

Hunter Cox made the second hole-in-one of his golfing career at Kempsville Meadows. Cox aced the 150-yard 14th hole with a six-iron.

July 16, 1968

Hunter aced his third hole-in-one.

December 4, 1974

Hunter gained his fourth hole-in-one at Cedar Point.

July 13, 1975

Hunter achieved his fifth hole-in-one.

There were good comments and best wishes from his friend and golf partner, W.B. Meredith, II, builder in Norfolk and Virginia Beach.

Two "Hole in One" trophies

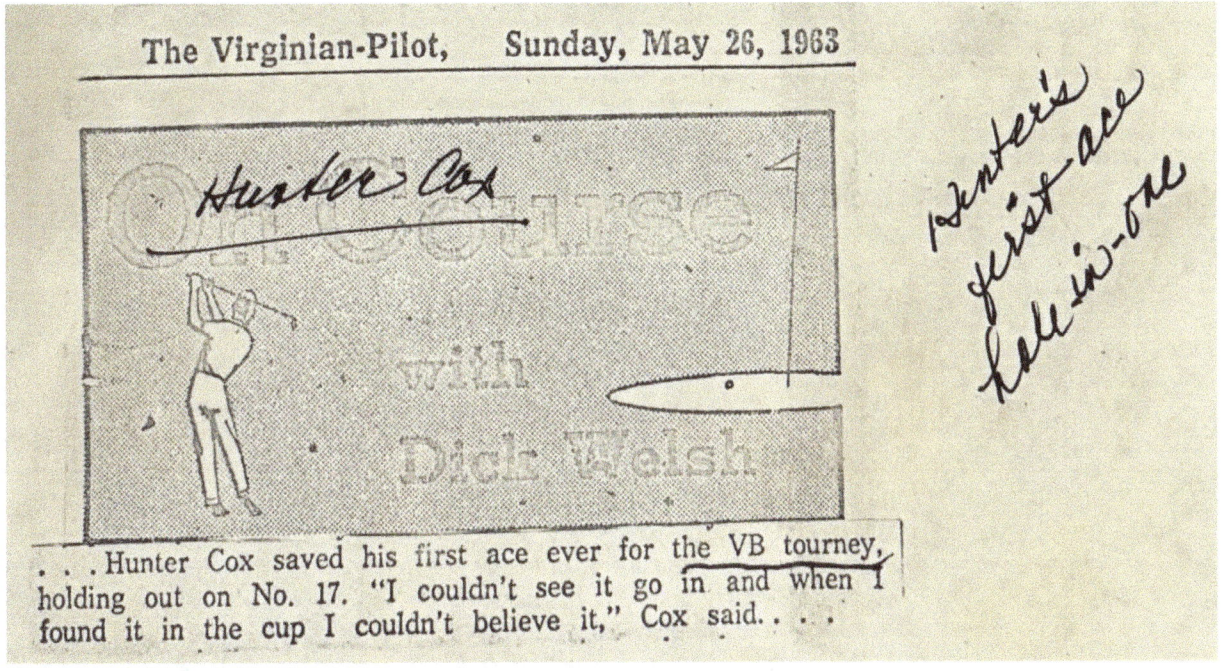

Hunter's First Hole-in-one

Local Golf Briefs

May 27, 1968

If Peninsula-area golfers become favorite visitors at future Princess Anne Country Club member-guest tournaments it will come as no surprise.

Two young men journeyed from the other side of Hampton Roads this weekend and helped their hosts take the first two places in this years event.

Moss Becroft of Newport News teamed with Waverly Berkley for a final-round 70 Sunday and a one-stroke win over Brad Tazewell and Sam Wallace of Williamsburg.

Berkley and Becroft had earlier rounds of 74 and 68 to finish with a 212 total.

W. F. Magann and Mrs. Frankie Bron won a scorecard playoff after four teams had tied for first with 67s in a mixed scotch foursome at Cedar Point Sunday.

Other teams in the tie included George Skinner and Mrs. Marguerite Whitehead, J. G. Sprigg and Mrs. Keith Baldwin and Bob Howell and Mrs. Anne Thurston.

Two teams finished with a best ball of 53 to tie for top honors in a mixed blitz at Eagle Haven yesterday. Lefty Wright, Helen Mitchell, Clark Jarvis and Wilma Vickery made up one foursome and Roger Smith, Doris Barek, A. D. Wyss and Joe Simcisko the other.

Hunter Cox made the second hole-in-one of his golfing career Sunday at Kempsville Meadows. Cox aced the 150-yard 14th hole with a six iron.

May 27, 1968

KEMPSVILLE — Hunter Cox scored a hole-in-one on the 14th hole at Kempsville Meadows Sunday. He sank a 6-iron shot on the 150-yard hole for his second ace. He aced the 17th at Kempsville seven years ago. His partners Sunday were Ed Gross, Bob Hassell, and Lou Taylor.

The Virginian-Pilot, 25
Monday, Oct. 9, 1967

Cox Wins Golf Cup With 71

NORFOLK — Hunter Cox shot a 78-7—71 to win the monthly President's Cup award in Tidewater Golf Association play at Lake Wright.

Cox teamed with Bob Fentress for a 143 best ball and first in the competition. One shot back were teams composed of Tom Nelson and Lew Taylor, and Steve Edwards and Tom Lawson.

Jack Lockman scored an ace on the 135-yard 16th hole, using an eight-iron.

CAVALIER (blind bogey 69)—Buddy Cole, 86-17; Billy Malbon, 86-17; Speedy Hutchins, 69-0.
EAGLE HAVEN (77)—Tom Roberts 77-0.
BOW CREEK (79)—Dave Jones, 84-5; Bill Black, 92-13; Bob Solvey, 94-15.
CEDAR POINT (78)—Hunter Rawlings, 91-13; A. T. Douglass, 90-12; W. C. Worthington, 83-5; Joe Bryant, 82-4; Pat Barham, 99-21.
BIDE-A-WEE (73)—Joe Ricketts, 87-14; Mack Copper, 85-12; Ervin Holsweig, 90-17.
DORSEY MEAD SCHOOL OF GOLF (blitz)—Leonard Austin, Roddy Bolanga.
KEMPSVILLE MEADOWS (mixed blitz)—Lillian Oliver, Dave Mondy, Monte Oden, Arnold Freeman, 58.
BOW CEEK (mixed blitz)—Virginia Opalio, Roger McMillan, George Owens Tom Shackelford, 23-28—51.

Oct 15 1965

Golf Meet Set At Stumpy Lake

NORFOLK — Play begins Saturday morning in the Stumpy Lake club golf championships. Thirty three players in three flights will compete in the 36-hole medal play.

Championship Flight
10—Jim Hunnicutt, Jim Pinkard, Wes Barham, Bobby Fentress. 10:05, Joe Ellen, Bob Edgerton, Henry Fluty, Jim Lombard. 10:10, Tim Douglass, Bill Hebert, Short Douglass, Bill Soday.

First Flight
10:15—Dr. Walt Summers, Al Todd, Hunter Cox, Dave Shackelford. 10:20, Red Burke, Carl Rhodes, Al Myers, Ed Gross. 10:25, Grady Ward, O. D. Izon, Walter Smith, Daryl Swin.

Second Flight
10:30—Skinny Porter, Carl Lambert, Ed Byrd, 10:35, John Garrett, Billy Tarrh, Fred Muzquiz. 10:40, Bob Spivey, Johnny Walker, Glen Small.

Chapter 8:
Norfolk Redevelopment & Housing Authority

Hunter with the Norfolk Redevelopment and Housing Authority

Hunter worked for the Norfolk Redevelopment and Housing Authority from 1959 to 1970, holding several key roles during his tenure. He began as a Land Disposition Agent, advanced to Assistant Director of Industrial Development, and ultimately became Director. The Authority's Executive Director during this period was Mr. Lawrence M. Cox (no relation to Hunter).

As Land Disposition Agent, Hunter oversaw the Authority's architectural, planning, and engineering functions. His responsibilities also included acquiring real estate, managing land sales, relocating families and businesses, and overseeing demolition operations.

Hunter's office was located on the 24th floor of the newly built Virginia National Bank Building, a high-rise in downtown Norfolk. During his time there, he spearheaded efforts to eliminate slums in Norfolk, replacing them with modern housing projects. He was instrumental in transforming Granby Street into a pedestrian mall. Hunter worked closely with Casey Holtzinger, a colleague in the drafting department who documented Norfolk's underserved communities through photographs and illustrations. Their friendship endured, and many of Holtzinger's watercolors now adorn Hunter's home.

In 1965, Hunter oversaw the construction of the Rotunda, a striking seven-story circular office building on St. Paul Boulevard, near St. Paul's Church. Standing 100 feet tall, the building was designed for rental office space. Under Hunter's leadership as Director of Industrial Development, Norfolk saw the removal of its notorious downtown slums, once considered some of the worst in the world. He orchestrated the demolition of outdated buildings, rows of sleazy, honky tonk establishments, and scandalous red-light districts catering to visiting sailors.

Hunter's efforts transformed Granby Street and revitalized Norfolk's housing developments. Among his notable achievements was the announcement of a $11 million Convention, Cultural, and Sports Center in July 1965. This development included the SCOPE complex, featuring a theater for performing arts and a hall accommodating 11,000 people. The project symbolized Norfolk's ambitious commitment to overcoming urban blight. Thanks in part to Hunter's leadership, Norfolk earned the prestigious All-America City Award in 1960, celebrating the city's successful revitalization efforts.

With a population of approximately 315,000 at the time, Norfolk had evolved from its earlier reputation as a "sleepy sailors' town" into a vibrant urban center. While it remained home to the Atlantic Fleet, the Fifth Naval District, NATO, and other federal installations, the city diversified its economy, with military and federal payrolls accounting for 40% of the area's income.

P. H. Cox, Jr.

May 12, 1960

Letter to Norfolk Redevelopment Housing Authority telling Mr. Lawrence Cox how much the residents of Grandy Park loved and praised young Hunter Cox. Hunter loved all of them and was interested in their problems too! Mr. Lawrence Cox let the residents know that Hunter's time at Grandy Park was for training purposes only. He must assume other duties at Norfolk Redevelopment Housing Authority.

HOPE CHAPEL
3406 Strathmore Ave.
Norfolk 4, Virginia

Mailing Address:
3762 Mississippi Avenue
Norfolk 2, Virginia

May 12, 1960

Mr. Lawrence Cox
National Bank Commerce Bldg.
Norfolk, Va.

Dear Mr. Cox:

May we add our commendation to those of the residents of Grandy Park in their praise of young H. P. Cox, Jr.!

They certainly love him! Little children call to him on the streets, and the older ones seem to watch for him to pass to hear his cheery greetings! He's seemed to have learned all of them already; both them and their problems! He's interested in each one!

He's the most amazing man of his young age it's been our pleasure to run up with in a long time! Just how he could have acquired so much understanding in such a short time is more than we can comprehend!

The funniest part of it all is how he gets the residents of the Park to conform to all the rules and do things they don't want to, and end up agreeing with him and liking him even more!

We're just fortunate in having a young man of his calibre dedicating his life to working with the less fortunate!

Best of wishes

Chas. and Helen Sousa

NORFOLK REDEVELOPMENT AND HOUSING AUTHORITY

CHAS. L. KAUFMAN, Chairman
JAMES E. ETHERIDGE, Vice-Chairman
MELVIN T. BLASSINGHAM
PRETLOW DARDEN
JOHN L. ROPER, 2ND

LAWRENCE M. COX
Executive Director

POST OFFICE BOX 968 - NORFOLK 1, VIRGINIA

NATIONAL BANK OF COMMERCE BUILDING

TELEPHONE MAdison 5-4501

May 16, 1960

Mrs. Helen Sousa
3762 Mississippi Avenue
Norfolk 2, Virginia

Dear Mrs. Sousa:

Thank you for your letter of May 12, 1960. Your letter of commendation of the ability and performance of our Mr. Hunter Cox is most gratifying.

We regret to tell you, however, that he cannot continue as the Housing Manager of Grandy Park, inasmuch as his assignment there was temporary and for training purposes only. Now that his training in the problems of Housing Management has been completed, he must assume other duties with the Authority.

Again we express our appreciation to you and through you to the tenants of Grandy Park for your joint interest in Mr. Cox.

Very truly yours,

Lawrence M. Cox
Executive Director

cc: Mr. P. H. Cox, II

RESIDENTS OF GRANDY PARK
NORFOLK, VA.

May 7, 1960

Mr. Lawrence Cox, mgr.
Norfolk Redevelopment and Housing
National Bank of Commerce
Norfolk, Va.

Dear Mr. Cox:

We, the residents of Grandy Park, want you to know how much we appreciate you sending us such a fine young man as our manager, namely, Mr. P. H. Cox, Jr.

He has endeared himself to all of us in this very short time!

He has acquainted himself with all of us, and our problems are his! However, this does not mean that he does not strictly conform to all Park rules! He does! Furthermore, he sees that we do! But he does it in such ways that we conform to things we dislike and even enjoy doing it for him!

We look for his happy face and cheery greetings as he constantly prods the streets of the Park! He's interested in each little child, the sufferings of our sick and aged and the problems of our younger residents!

There must be a great future for this young man and we would not for a minute wish to interfere with it, but could you spare him to us for a while longer? This, of course, if it meets with his approval!

Thank you so very much.

Respectfully,
Residents of Grandy Park

Tidewater Virginia Development Council (TVDC)

After leaving the Norfolk Redevelopment and Housing Authority, Hunter continued his career with Mayor Fred W. Duckworth at the Tidewater Virginia Development Council (TVDC). Hunter also completed courses at the Philadelphia Real Estate School, at the University of Richmond, at the Virginia Real Estate School, and at the Harvard School of Business Administration.

Chesapeake hires away TVDC man

CHESAPEAKE — Parke Hunter Cox Jr., industrial development manager for the Tidewater Virginia Development Council, will go to work full-time for the city of Chesapeake Aug. 1.

The city will pay him $18,480 to start, and his job will be to direct Chesapeake's industrial development program.

"He is most highly qualified," City Manager G. R. House Jr. told the Chesapeake City Council in announcing Cox's appointment Tuesday afternoon.

Cox has been with TVDC for a year.

Before that, he spent 10 years with the Norfolk Redevelopment Housing Authority, rising from administrative aide to director of development.

Cox holds two degrees, an A.B. in history and a B.S. in political science, from Hampden-Sydney College.

Later, he completed courses at the Philadelphia Real Estate School (in real estate appraisal), at the University of Richmond (in labor relations), at the Virginia Real Estate School (in real estate dealing) and at the Harvard School of Business Administration (in advanced management).

He is a member of the Virginia Club, the Commonwealth Club, the Norfolk Rotary Club and the Masons, and he is a past president of both the Tidewater and Stumpy Lake Golf Associates.

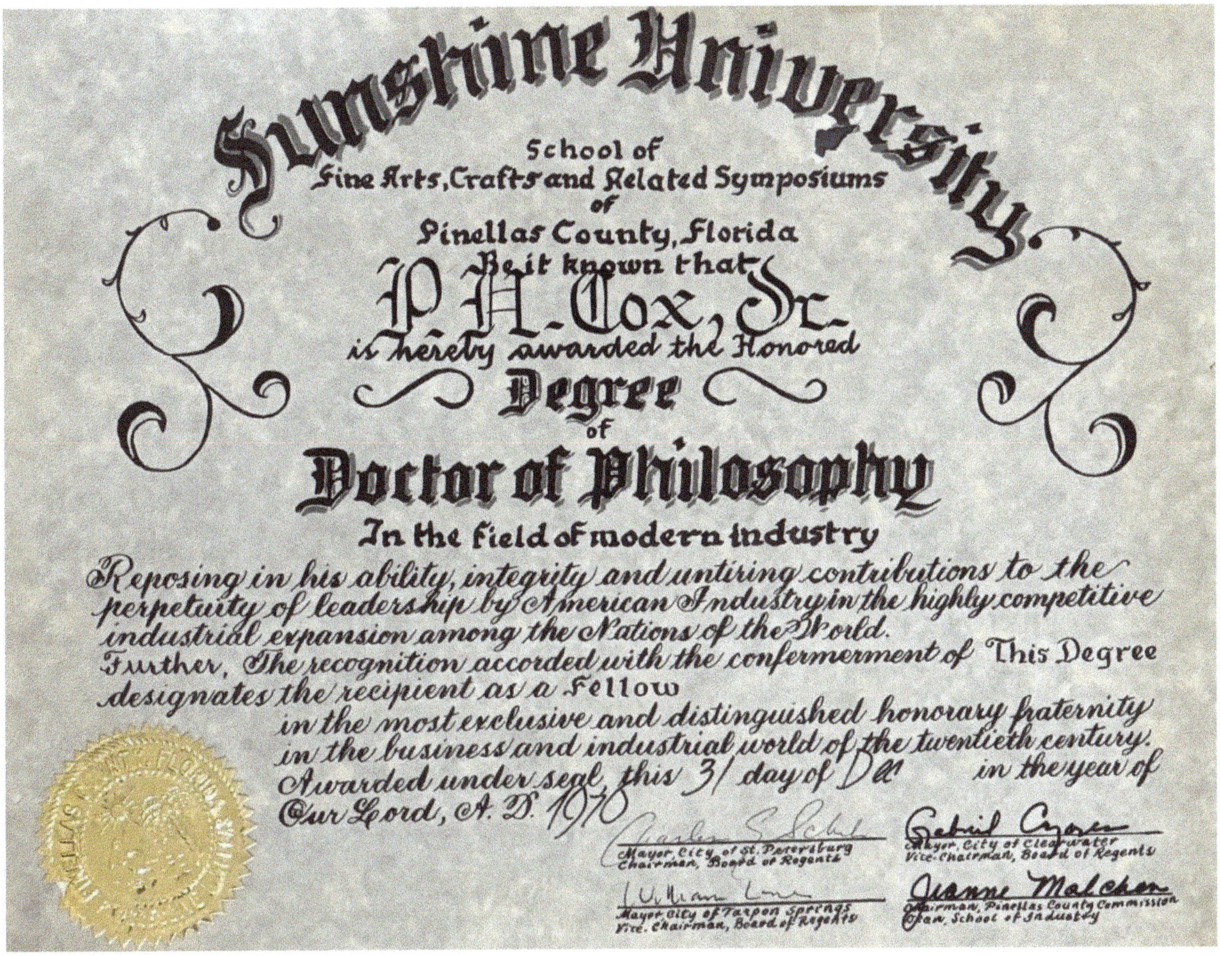
Sunshine University
School of
Fine Arts, Crafts and Related Symposiums
of
Pinellas County, Florida
Be it known that
P. H. Cox, Sr.
is hereby awarded the Honored
Degree
of
Doctor of Philosophy
In the field of modern industry

Reposing in his ability, integrity and untiring contributions to the perpetuity of leadership by American Industry in the highly competitive industrial expansion among the Nations of the World.
Further, The recognition accorded with the confermement of This Degree designates the recipient as a Fellow in the most exclusive and distinguished honorary fraternity in the business and industrial world of the twentieth century.
Awarded under seal this 31 day of Dec in the year of Our Lord, A. D. 1970

Mayor, City of St. Petersburg
Chairman, Board of Regents

Mayor, City of Clearwater
Vice-Chairman, Board of Regents

Mayor, City of Tarpon Springs
Vice-Chairman, Board of Regents

Jeanne Malchon
Chairman, Pinellas County Commission
Dean, School of Industry

An inside joke among Hunter & his colleagues

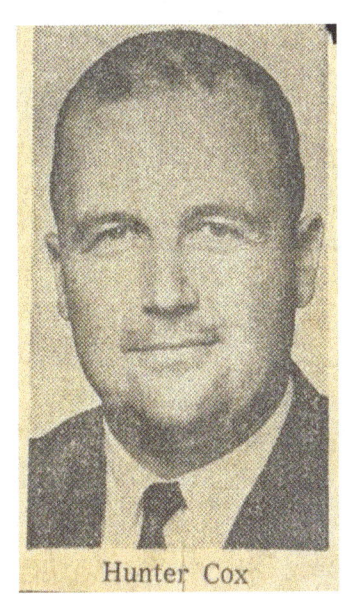

Hunter Cox

Chapter 9:
Director of Industrial Development for the City of Chesapeake

B2 The Ledger-Star, Saturday, Feb. 9, 1980

Smooth-talking industry hunter

A tribute to the City of Chesapeake and its Industrial Development Department

Chesapeake's Attitude
POSITIVE

Chesapeake thrives on positive attitude... and the positive action it produces. Take industrial development, for instance. Chesapeake has a national reputation for concentrated, positive effort directed toward the development of industrial facilities.

As your hometown newspaper, the CHESAPEAKE POST speaks for a proud and positive community when we say we are glad to have each and every new industry added to Chesapeake's growing list of prestigious industrial firms.

As your partner in the progress and the future of Chesapeake, the POST will be with you all the way. We'll report, photograph and applaud your events and your achievements.

And the POST offers a special salute to the Chesapeake Industrial Development Authority, to P. H. Cox Jr. and the Industrial Development Department for an outstanding contribution to the positive growth of Chesapeake.

Chesapeake Post

"Working to build Chesapeake"

Hunter was a very prominent part of the growth of Chesapeake, VA. He bridged the gap between various companies and the city of Chesapeake.

Hunter standing on the left with councilmen of Chesapeake, VA

$165 million Chesapeake industrial expansion eyed

By JOHN LEVIN

CHESAPEAKE — Stockholders, your investment in Chesapeake industrial development is turning up blue chips.

The annual report to citizens by the city's Industrial Development Department indicates that 41 businesses have decided to locate or expand their operations here.

They will invest a total of $165,411,000 in new buildings, machinery and equipment which will mean $2,430,635 more in real estate and personal property tax revenue to the city.

The figures are from P. Hunter Cox Jr., director of Chesapeake's Industrial Development office.

Cox's board room jargon likens Chesapeake citizens to stockholders. Their company is the Industrial Development Department and their investment is public money in the future of the city as an industrial center.

The citizen-stockholders are entitled to an annual report on the department's activities, Cox said.

The report measures the department's work for an August to July year and is usually mailed to every Chesapeake householder in early December.

This year's report is compiled and ready to be published but because of delays in the city's print shop, the finished report won't be distributed until February.

The report will show that 1971-74 has been the most successful for the four-year-old department. Its efforts should realize 4,518 more jobs in addition to boosting the city's tax base.

Volvo, the North American subsidiary of the Swedish auto manufacturer announced this year it would build the first foreign auto manufacturing operation in the United States in Chesapeake's Greenbrier Industrial area.

Volvo will spend $250 million on the auto assembly plant and plans to employ 3,300 people.

In addition, Volvo's marine engine subsidiary, Volvo Penta of America Inc. will invest $700,000 in a facility to market, sell, distribute and service marine and industrial engines here. That operation will employ 50 people.

Also the company is now erecting a new car sales facility at Greenbrier. The dealership will represent a $1 million investment and employ 30 people.

Cox's report also notes the merger of the Norfolk Southern Railway into the Southern Railway System last January as important to Chesapeake's industrial development.

He cited the relocation of the railroad's headquarters from Portsmouth's Pinner's Point area to Chesapeake.

Other industrial development cited in the report includes:

★ Bissette Construction Corp. $120,000 investment, to employ 10 persons, concrete products manufacturer relocated from Norfolk.

★ Branham Electric Corp. $100,000 investment, to employ 35 persons, electrical contractors relocated from Virginia Beach.

★ Bullington Distributing Company, $150,000 investment, to employ 10 persons, exporter and importer.

★ L. R. Capshaw Inc., $1,-070,000 investment, to employ 22 persons, oil terminal.

★ Chesapeake Auto Truck Repair, $50,000 expansion, to employ 9 additional persons.

★ Commonwealth Natural Gas Corp., $10,000 expansion, no new employes.

★ Eagle Transportation Co., $250,000 investment, to employ 15 persons.

★ Elizabeth River Terminals Inc., $2,760,000 investment, to employ 50 persons.

★ Environmental Recycling Corp., $40,000 investment, to employ six persons.

★ Eure Rentals Inc., $2,000 expansion, no new employes.

★ G and S Equipment Corp. Inc., $30,000 expansion, no new employes.

★ Givens Inc., $30,000 investment to relocate from Norfolk, no new employes.

★ Griffin Wellpoint Corp., $7,000 expansion, two new employes.

★ H and M Contracting Co., $150,000 expansion, no new employes.

★ Huggerno-Buchanan Inc., $500,000 relocation from another part of the city, 25 new employes.

★ Ireland Equipment Co., $150,000 investment, two new employes.

★ Kenan Transport Co., $25,000 expansion, four new employes.

★ Kline Chevrolet Sales Corp., $1,150,000 investment, 150 employes, relocation from Norfolk.

★ Life Federal Savings and Loan Assn., $250,000 investment in new branch office, to employ six persons.

★ Lone Star Industries Inc., $1 million expansion of its block and pipe plant, to employ 50 persons.

★ National Structural System, $300,000 investment, to employ 35 persons to manufacture precast concrete slabs.

★ Oil Equipment Sales and Service Co. Inc., $65,000 investment in relocation, 17 employes.

★ Oil Transport Inc., $250,000 expansion, 30 employes.

★ Old Dominion Steel Co., $150,000 investment, 16 employes.

★ Portsmouth Trailer Sales, $100,000 investment in relocation, 10 employes.

★ Security U Stor and Lock, $600,000 investment, 3 employes.

★ Service Disposal Corp., $300,000 investment in relocation from Norfolk, 14 employes.

★ Southland Cork Co., $26,000 expansion, 20 employes.

★ Zack V. Taft Co., Inc., $300,000 investment, relocation from Virginia Beach, asphalt manufacturer, 150 employes.

★ Tidewater Dispose-All Inc. $200,000 investment, relocation from Norfolk, 40 employes.

★ Tidewater Battery Co., $150,000 investment, relocation, eight employes.

★ Tidewater Fibre Corp., $450,000 investment, 30 employes, collection of waste paper for recycling.

★ Vico Construction Corp., $170,000 investment, 30 employes.

★ Virginia Engine Ltd. $250,000 investment, eight employes.

★ Virginia Precast Corp., $1 million investment, 50 employes, manufacturer of precast sewer structures.

★ Williams Crane and Rigging Co. Inc., $200,000 investment, 35 employes.

★ Yale Industrial Trucks-Richmond Inc., $150,000 investment, 12 employes.

★ Radio Station WJLY, $100,000 investment, 12 employes.

Cox said announcement of Volvo's decision to locate in Chesapeake has established the city as an industrial center.

He said other industries will now be interested in the city much the way merchants want to locate near other stores in shopping centers.

He predicted the industrial growth of Chesapeake will now occur in geometric progression; one industry attracts two others, two industries attract four more and so on.

Cox also credited citizen attitude for the city's industrial growth. He said people here accept and welcome new industry.

COX

P. Hunter Cox Jr. is instrumental in such projects as the Greenbrier Mall, the first regional shopping center in the city, which will open this fall.

Chesapeake Has Room For Its Growing Future

Now 10 years old, Chesapeake has matured from an adolescent city into an adult that is rapidly filling out with new residential and unprecedented industrial and commercial growth.

Born in 1963 through the merger of Norfolk County with South Norfolk, Chesapeake's once-rural population grew by 30,000 during the 1970s to its present census count of about 112,000.

Accompanying the population growth are homes, shopping centers, and industrial parks which city planners say will make Chesapeake a regional commerce center for the 1980s.

While other Hampton Roads cities are running out of land for development, Chesapeake boasts an area of 351 square miles, much of which is undeveloped and leaves potential for continued growth during the decade.

This fall, the doors will open to the 300-million Greenbrier Mall, the city's first regional shopping center, which will have 116 stores.

Two major highways, I-64 and the Great Bridge Bypass, are nearing completion and will be counted on to accommodate expected heavier traffic in the 80s.

Last year the Army Corps of Engineers finished dredging an extension of the deep water channel of the Southern Branch of the Elizabeth River. The project opened up about 400 acres of undeveloped land to industries dependent on access to water transportation.

The city's first water treatment plant, completed last March, is pumping nearly 10 million gallons daily, relieving Chesapeake of most of its former dependence on Norfolk and Portsmouth to provide drinking water.

A $2.3-million building on the Chesapeake campus of Tidewater Community College opened in 1980, housing classes for 1,500 students who were had to attend classes in temporary facilities.

The city seems to be gathering momentum for 1981. Industrial development may be the brightest prospect, many new firms, and some old companies from Norfolk and Portsmouth, are moving to Chesapeake because of the availability of land, utilities, and low tax rates.

In the year ending July 31, 1980, 32 industries either settled in Chesapeake or expanded facilities, investing a total of $33.5 million and offering 879 new jobs.

Of the firms, 13 were new to Chesapeake, offering 532 jobs and an investment of $29.1 million, and 19 firms expanded with an investment of $4 million and employment for 347 more residents.

Industrial development director P. Hunter Cox Jr. expects the growth to continue through the 1980s. For 1981, he predicts the expansion of many industries in Chesapeake but expects few new firms to move to the city because of the recession.

The City Council early this year will consider developing an industrial park on a 527-acre site in Greenbrier to accommodate growth. Chesapeake has two other major industrial parks, Cavalier Industrial Park in Deep Creek has about 200 acres left for expansion. Another park, also located in Greenbrier, has run out of space late in 1980.

Cox describes most of the industries as "nonpolluting types."

Among the largest firms in Chesapeake are Huggerno-Buchanan Inc., a heavy construction company; Wayne-chester Corp., which manufactures vinyl siding; Smith Douglass Division of Borden Chemical, which produces fertilizers; Southland Industries, Inc., which makes automotive and industrial gaskets; and Plasser American Corp., which makes machinery for the maintenance of railroad tracks.

Volvo, the Swedish automobile manufacturer, built an assembly line on a 530-acre tract in Greenbrier during the mid-1970s. The corporation hopes one day to begin producing cars at the site. The company is used only to prepare imported cars for shipment to dealers throughout the United States and to add optional equipment ordered by buyers. It employs about 130 people. The plant was designed to produce 80,000 cars a year and employ 3,000.

Construction may begin in 1981 on a $200-million oil refinery if Sunoco Oil Co. is granted a permit by the Environmental Protection Agency. The EPA is expected to rule on the permit this winter. The refinery would be built in the Gilmerton industrial area off South Military Highway.

The City Council is hoping to complement industrial development by attracting more small businesses to Chesapeake and Mayor Sidney M. Oman appointed a task force last summer for that purpose. The task force is surveying existing businesses to determine their attitudes about Chesapeake.

The city's real estate tax is 96 cents per $100 of assessed value. City assessments on real estate increased from $1.7 billion in 1979 to $1.3 billion in 1980.

School enrollment has decreased slightly in recent years, but officials believe the decline has leveled off. They anticipate increases in the next few years.

The public school system has 33 schools, 20 of them elementary. A high school in Great Bridge and an elementary school in Western Branch will be built within the next few years.

The median family income has climbed to $16,028, almost doubling in a decade and putting Chesapeake second only to Virginia Beach in South Hampton Roads.

The unemployment rate is 5.7 percent, the average for the area.

Agriculture is still the largest business in Chesapeake, with more than $12 million worth of farm products sold annually.

Jamaica

Hunter and I traveled to Jamaica in search of industries for Chesapeake. In 1971, Hunter successfully brought Tropigas International Corp., located at 2151 Le Jeune Rd., Coral Gables, FL 33134, to Chesapeake. In gratitude for his efforts, the company gifted us a trip to Kingston, Jamaica.

On August 6, 1971, we flew to Montego Bay and stayed at the Tower Isle Hotel in Ocho Rios. It was a particularly memorable experience for me—it was not only my first time flying but also my birthday. After 14 years of marriage, this trip marked our very first vacation together. It was truly a wonderful and unforgettable journey!

Book of matches from Jamaica

TROPIGAS INTERNATIONAL CORP.
2151 LE JEUNE ROAD
CORAL GABLES, FLORIDA 33134

July 20, 1971

Mr. Hunter Cox
Director Industrial Development
City of Chesapeake
Post Office Box 15225
Chesapeake, Virginia 23320

Dear Hunter:

I am enclosing your airline tickets. Mr. M. A. (Joe) Henry who is our division manager of Tropical Gas Company, Inc. in Kingston, Jamaica has advised me by letter that all reservations and arrangements have been made and you and Mrs. Cox will be staying at the Tower Isles in Ocho Rios. Incidentally, Joe Henry's office telephone number in Kingston is 936-2190 and the assistant manager's name is Don Hines.

Please sign for all meals, etc. at Tower Isles and, I believe, there are inter-locking arrangements with the other hotels in Ocho Rios which will permit dining elsewhere and charging the Tower Isles.

As previously indicated, Joe Henry will have someone meet your EAL Flight 995 at Montego Bay upon arrival August 6.

I will be in touch with you, however, before then.

With all kind regards and best wishes, I am

Cordially,

Robert E. Gresimer

REG:jm

Enclosures

Jamaica's invite

79

Inside our hotel in Jamaica

On the beach in Jamaica drinking coconut water

P. H. Cox, director of the Department of Industrial Development in Chesapeake places another Chesapeake flag, representing a new company on the locations map of Chesapeake. The department has been in operations for one year and during that year, new business and local expansions, valued at over $22 million dollars, have begun operations in Chesapeake.

Hunter's office was a modest 12-by-16-foot cedar block in South Norfolk, but its size didn't hinder his work—or the efficiency of his secretary, Mrs. Griffin. Despite the cramped quarters, Ms. Griffin cheerfully answered calls and managed the office with precision.

The small office didn't stop Hunter from achieving big results. He facilitated more than $17 million in industrial investments, creating over 500 jobs. A lay committee noted that the annual tax revenue generated by those industries amounted to $260,000. They concluded that the man serving as the city's first point of contact for industrial executives deserved a more fitting office environment.

Hunter, however, had a solution of his own. He made sure to meet industrial clients before they reached his office, escorting them in the city's spacious automobile to tour potential development sites—allowing Chesapeake's opportunities to speak for themselves.

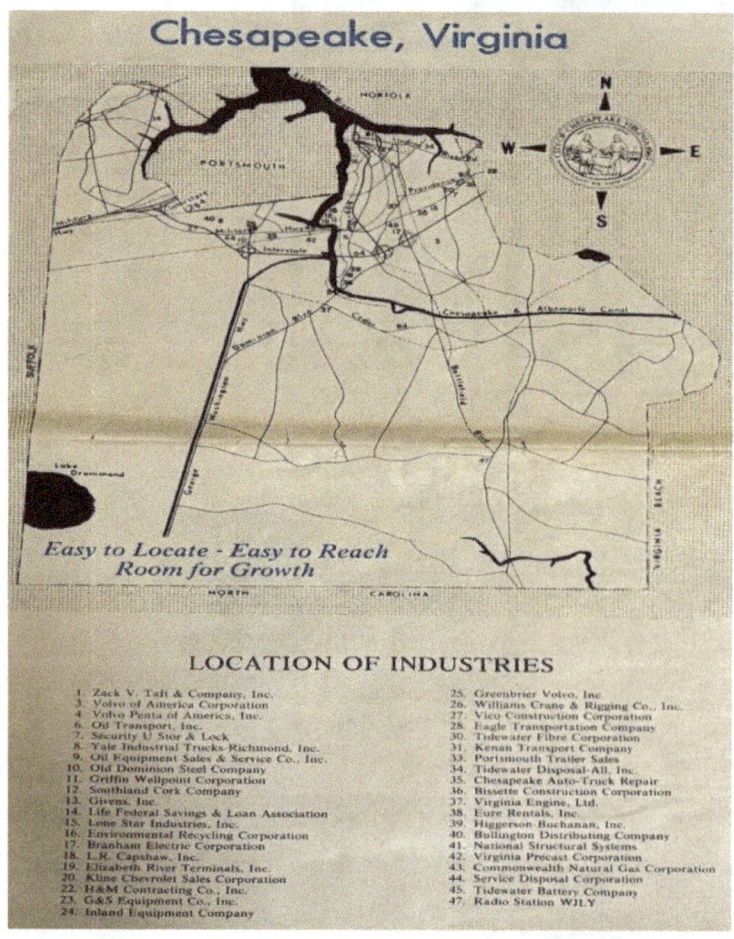

Thank you...

The activities of the Industrial Development Authority of the City of Chesapeake have increased as it continues to give aid and assistance in the financing of Chesapeake industries through Industrial Development Revenue Bond issues. Our appreciation is extended to this body of dedicated citizens.

As we look back on what has to be our finest year to date, we look forward City officials and all of our Stockholders, the Citizens of Chesapeake, we thank you for your never ending support of our Industrial Development Program. to even greater years ahead. To the City Council, clubs, organizations,

P.H. Cox, Jr.

Director of Industrial Development

Published by:
Industrial Development Department
1205 - 20th Street
Chesapeake, Virginia 23324
Telephone: 804-545-6029 or 545-6262

Photos by:
Fred Habit Photography Studio

INDUSTRIAL DEVELOPMENT AUTHOR

H. Leon Hodges — Chairman
Robert S. Bass — Vice-Chairman
Paul F. Rule — Secretary-Treasur
Walter Cartwright, Jr.
Joseph D. Choate
R. E. Grissom

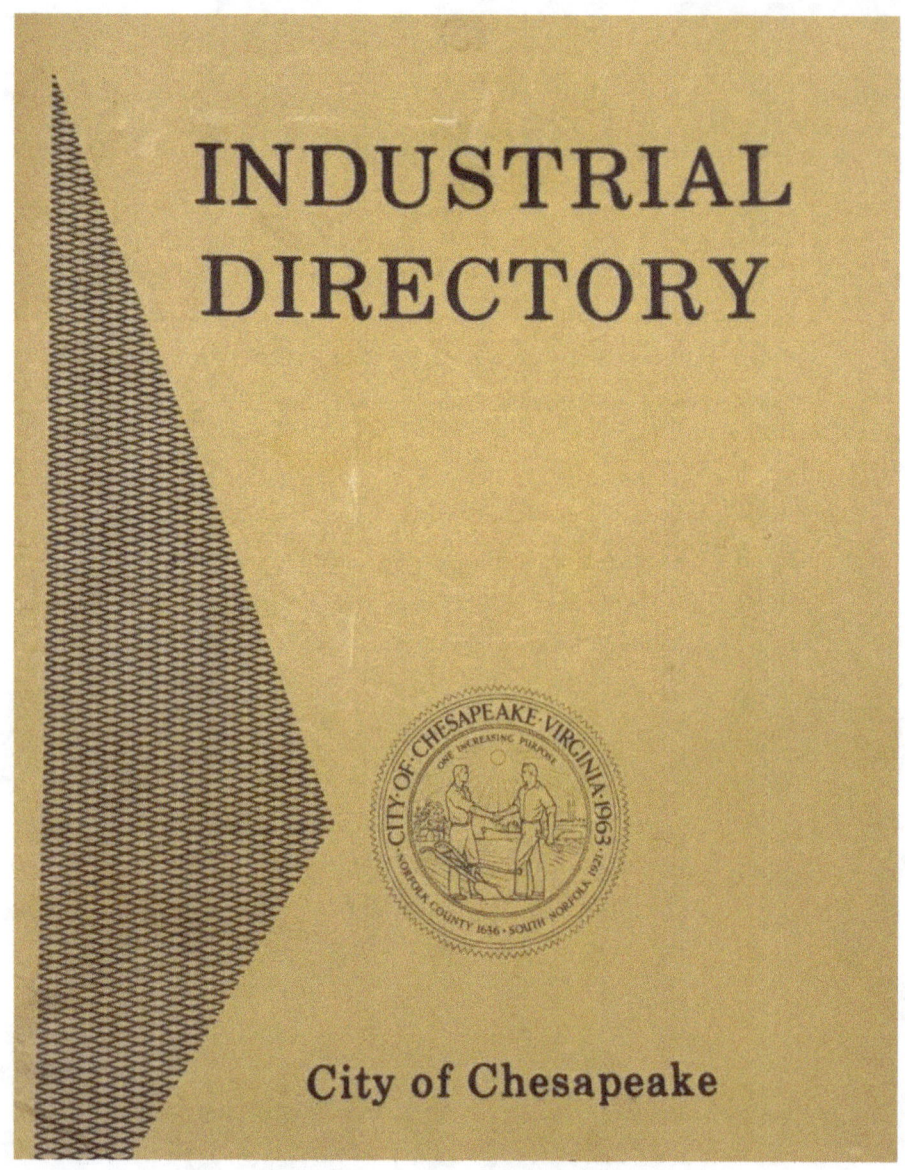

From the years 1971-1984 Hunter employed and brought 7,380 jobs to the people of Chesapeake. The Industrial Directory for the City of Chesapeake in 1975 list 291 new industries that came to Chesapeake.

City of Chesapeake Industrial Development Director Hunter Cox says accommodations for easy importing /exporting by rail, sea, and air have placed Chesapeake in the national and international industrial markets. Hunter worked as Director of Industrial Development for the City of Chesapeake from 1970-1983 then he retired at 47 years of age.

A list of plants and industries and their investments follows:

1969-1970

- Alcoa Aluminum

$1.5 Million

- Commonwealth Natural Sas

$7.5 Million

- Trapigas International

$4.6 Million

- Bruce Paseling and Molding

$3.5 Million

Plasser American Corporation

$500.000

- Evans Molding Plant

$3 Million

- Lone Star- Le Farge

$3 Million

- Atlantic Energy (Combination of Trapizas and Commonwealth Gas)

$6 Million

1972- 1973

- Foster Grant

$15 Million

A list of plants and industries and their investments follows:

1972-73

- Bay Ware Housing (expansion)

$1 Million

- Evans Plant (expansion)

$2,75 Million

- Cavalier Ford (relocation)

$850,000

- Columbia Yacht (relocation)

$3 Million

- Chesapeake Campus Tidewater Community College

$2.5 Million

Cox said, "The location of Volvo, Foster Grant, Alcos, Bruce Paneling and Molding Co, Evans Products, and Plasser American Corporation brought a higher caliber of residents into the city and 769 new jobs."

List of the industries Hunter brought to Chesapeake, VA:

1. 84 Lumber Company
2. A&P Waters Sewer Supplies, Inc
3. Agency Rent A Car
4. Albemarle Supply Co. Inc
5. Aldo Construction Corp.
6. Allen, I. J., & Son
7. Aluminum Co. of America
8. Alpha Beta Construction
9. Amigo Sales of Va.
10. Amoco Oil Company
11. American Electric Co.
12. American Hardware & Home
13. American Hoechst Company
14. American Hospital Supply

15. American Oil Company
16. American Phone Service Company
17. Arbor Landscaping, Inc.
18. Armour and Company
19. Art Lite Sign Company
20. Asphalt Paving
21. AT&T Information System
22. Atlantic Cement Co.
23. Atlantic Energy, Inc.
24. Atlantic Richfield
25. Atlantic Roofing Service
26. Atlantic Yacht Basin
27. Austin Electric Company
28. Aztec Technical Corp.
29. B&B Hose & Rubber Co., Inc.
30. Bank of Virginia - Tide Water
31. Barakey Medical Building
32. Barnum-Bruns Iron Works
33. Battaglia Produce Ship.
34. Bay Warehouses, Inc.
35. Baynor Furniture
36. Bayville Farms, Inc.
37. Be Miss Equipment Corporation
38. Betterton & Whitlow
39. Billy's Heating, Cooling
40. Bissette Construction
41. Black Brothers Builders

42. Blue & Gray Transp. Co.
43. Bowman Transportation
44. Bralley-Willett Tank
45. Branham Electric Corp.
46. Brentwood Mini Storage
47. Brooks Electric Co., Inc.
48. Brown, E. W., Pl. & Htg.
49. Brownings Marine, Inc.
50. Bruce Paneling & Molding
51. Bryant, K. L., Plb. & Htg.
52. Bullington Distrib. Co.
53. Burton Lumber Company
54. Byerly Publications - The Chesapeake Post
55. Canal Ready Mix
56. Capital Equipment Company, Inc.
57. Cargill, Inc.
58. Cardinal Building Corporation
59. Carpenter Construction Co, Inc.
60. Carbonic Industrial Pack
61. Carnation Building Corporation
62. Celuka Plant
63. Central Italian Ices
64. Centrone's Italian Ices
65. Ceylon Tankers, Inc.
66. Chesapeake Auto-Truck
67. Chesapeake Bldg. Mtls.
68. Chesapeake Energy Center - VEPCO

69. Chesapeake Equipment
70. Chesapeake Flooring, Co.
71. Chesapeake Furniture Manufacturing Corp.
72. Chesapeake Municipal Airport
73. Chesapeake Plb. Sply.
74. Chesapeake Post-Byerly
75. Chesapeake Propeller
76. Chesapeake Ready-Mix
77. Chesapeake Warehouse
78. Cherry, Palmer
79. Chilean Nitrate Sales
80. Citadel Cement
81. City Auto Supply
82. Colonial Pipe Line
83. Columbia Yacht
84. Commercial Recycling Corporation
85. Commonwealth Natural Gas Corporation
86. Commonwealth SNG, Inc.
87. Conrad Bros., Inc.
88. Continental Oil Co.
89. Cotton Young Insurance Agency
90. Crystal Wholesale Co.
91. Davidson Transfer & Storage
92. Davis Grain Corp.
93. Deep Creek Airport
94. Delro
95. Deltoid Truck Corp.

96. Deming Supply Company
97. Detterman's Furniture
98. Diamond G.M.C., Inc.
99. Diamond Hill Plywood Corporation
100. Dixie Farms
101. Dixie Sanitary Serv.
102. Divers, Dawley Sanade & Lassiter, Inc.
103. Dozier Tank & Welding Company
104. Dr. Tucker's Office Building
105. Dudley Construction
106. Dunlo Elec. Welding
107. D.D. Jones Transfer & Warehouse, Co. Inc
108. Eagle Transportation
109. Earle's Market
110. Eastern Fence & Awning
111. Eastern International
112. Eastern Leasing
113. Eastern Motor Transp.
114. Eden Square Office Condominiums
115. Ecolochem, Inc.
116. Ecology Services
117. Eight-Four Lumber Co.
118. Electric Motor & Contracting Co., Inc.
119. Elizabeth Pines Terminals, Inc.
120. Elizabeth River Terminals
121. Emco Electronics
122. Engineering Media

123. Environmental Recycling
124. Eppinger & Russell
125. Ernst, E.C., Inc.
126. Eure Rentals, Inc.
127. Evans Products Co.
128. Everett Express, Inc.
129. Exxon
130. Fiberglass Products
131. Fire Equipment Eng.
132. Forrest Septic Tank
133. Forsty More Meats
134. Foster Grant Co., Inc.
135. Friedman, M., Welding
136. Franasiate, Frank, M.D.
137. Fred Habit Photography Studio
138. G & S Equipment
139. GFM. Plasser American Corporation
140. Gentry Realty, Inc.
141. Giant Opera Air Market
142. Ginen's Inc.
143. Glass Craft, Inc.
144. Goebel American Web Products
145. Goodman Segar-Hogan
146. Gordon Paper Co.
147. Gowen Chemical Corp.
148. Gray & Curling Equip.
149. Great Bridge Block & Lbr.

150. Great Bridge Decorating
151. Greenbrier Volvo, Inc.
152. Griffin Wellpoint Corporation
153. Gulf Oil Company
154. G & M Tank Lines of Va., Inc.
155. H & H Heating & A/C
156. H & M Contracting Co., Inc.
157. Habit, Fred, Photography
158. Hair & Underwood
159. Halton Enterprises
160. Hanna Garden Center, Inc.
161. Harce Products, Inc.
162. Haywood's House of Pictures
163. Heath Contracting
164. Heath, DeFore's & Heath
165. Henrico Development Company
166. Herbst, Julius T., Inc.
167. Hillegass Lighting Corporation
168. Hilti Corporation
169. Hilti Fastening Systems
170. Higgerson-Buchanan, Inc.
171. Hobart Corporation
172. Hoffman Industries, Inc.
173. Hogan Diesel Service
174. Howell's Motor Freight, Inc.
175. Industrial Flooring Co.
176. Industrial Hardware & Supply

177. Inland Equipment Co.
178. Intercoastal Steel Corporation
179. Interior Systems of Virginia, Inc.
180. Ingram, Fred, Htg. & A/C
181. Jacobson Metal Company
182. J & L Distributing, Inc.
183. J. Underwater & Co., Inc.
184. Jefal Corporation
185. Johnson's Srip Propeller Rebuilding Corp.
186. Jones, D.D., Transfer
187. Jones & Frank Oil Eqpt.
188. Keeton Florist
189. Kenan Transport Co.
190. Kitchin Equipment
191. Kline Chevrolet Sales
192. Krisp Pak Co., Inc.
193. Lambert, R. D., & Son
194. Lawrence, R. E., & Co.
195. Lighting & Elec. Supply
196. Life Federal Savings & Loan
197. Liverman, Inc.
198. Lone Star Industries
199. Lowe's Companies, Inc.
200. Lowe's of Chesapeake, Inc.
201. Lucey, John D., Plb./Htg.
202. Luck Office Building
203. L. B. Foster Company

204. L. R. Capshaw, Inc.
205. M & M Tank Hires of Va., Inc.
206. Malpass Construction
207. Marco Products, Inc.
208. Marshall Electric
209. Master Auto Service Corporation
210. Matty Warehouse
211. Max-Ward Delmar Studios, Inc.
212. McCallum Inspection Co.
213. McCallum Testing Lab.
214. McDaniels Roofing Corp.
215. McLean Trucking
216. McPherson, H. R.
217. Meixel Meat Packing
218. Mercury Airways, Inc.
219. Mercury Motor Express
220. Midland Petroleum
221. Mid-Atlantic Leasing Corporation
222. Mid-Atlantic Video Tape Services, Inc.
223. Mid-Eastern Airways, Inc.
224. Miles, J. A., Flooring
225. Miles, J. D., & Sons
226. Minute Man Fuels
227. Mobil Oil Corporation
228. Modular Space Systems
229. Monroe Systems for Business
230. Moore's Super Stores

231. Moretrench American
232. Morgan Mill Works
233. Morris Coffee & Vending Company
234. Morris Company, Inc.
235. Multi-Metro Signs & Design
236. National Awning Manufacturing Co., Inc.
237. National Structural Sys.
238. Nelson & Smith
239. Nettles, T.E., Plbg.
240. N & W Railway Co. Portlock Yard
241. Norfolk Banana Dist.
242. Norfolk Dredging Company
243. Norfolk Tallow Co., Inc.
244. North Carolina National Bank Building
245. North State Motor Lines
246. O'Boyle Tank Lines
247. Oil Eqpt. Sales & Serv.
248. Oil Transport, Inc.
249. Old Dominion Freight
250. Old Dominion Steel
251. Old Dominion Sugar Company
252. Old Dominion Trucking Leasing
253. Oliver Septic Tank
254. Overnite Transportation
255. P & W Supply Corp.
256. Parkwood Douze, Inc.
257. Paul's Place

258. Patrick Coal Co.
259. Piedmont Petroleum
260. Phillips Petroleum
261. Poplar Hill Professional Center
262. Portlock Electric
263. Portsmouth Concrete
264. Portsmouth Trailer Sales
265. Pre-Fab Transit Co.
266. Priddy, Chas. W., & Co.
267. Princess Anne Equipment Corporation
268. Princess Anne Pile & Lbr.
269. Quality Controls, Inc.
270. Radio Station WCPK
271. Radio Station WJLY
272. Railway Express Agency
273. R & L Machine Shop
274. RCS Electric
275. Rea Construction Company
276. Regency Oldsmobile Inc.
277. Rental Tools & Equipment
278. Rhodes, W. L., Plb. & Htg.
279. Richardson Ornamental
280. Riviera Kitchens
281. Riverside Metal Works
282. Roadway Express, Inc.
283. Rogers Term. & Ship.
284. Royster Company

285. Russo & Mastracco Shopping Center
286. Sadler Materials
287. Safety Kleen
288. Sampson Services, Inc.
289. Schwerman Trucking
290. Security Fence Co.
291. Security U Store & Lock
292. Semca Truck Line
293. Service Disposal Corporation
294. Servisoft of Virginia
295. Shaffner Industries of Virginia, Inc.
296. Shell Oil Company
297. Sherwin-Williams Co.
298. Simmons & Son Roofing
299. Simpson Transfer & Stor.
300. Simpson Van & Whse.
301. Smith, Whitlaw Company
302. Smith & Keene Electric Service
303. Smith-Douglass
304. So. States Ches. Coop.
305. So. States Coop. (Fertlz.)
306. So. States Coop. Petrol.
307. Soil & Mtl. Engineers
308. Solite Masonry Units
309. Southland Cork Company
310. Southern Br. Yacht Basin
311. Southern Office Supply

312. Southern Overseas Corporation
313. Southern Packing
314. Southern Railway Company
315. Southern Railway System
316. Sprinkle Masonry
317. Spruill, W. E., Inc.
318. Stack House, Inc.
319. St. Joe Paper Company
320. Standard Parts Corporation
321. Standard Trucking Company
322. Stoneland Corp.
323. Stevenson Ford Tractor, Inc.
324. Stillman, L. E., Jr.
325. Sumner, Van, Inc.
326. Sunshine Biscuits
327. Superior Equipment Sales, Inc.
328. Superior Trucking Co.
329. Swann Chesapeake Terminal Corporation
330. Swift Chemical Co.
331. Tabor, J. W., & Son
332. Tacor Marise, Inc.
333. Taft, Zack V., & Co.
334. Tarabochia Marine Hydraulics Co., Inc.
335. Taylor Drapery & Carpet
336. Taylor Freezer Sales Company, Inc.
337. Temple, A. W., Inc.
338. Tenneco Oil Co.

339. Terminal Whse. & Ship.
340. Texaco Oil Company
341. Thurston Motor Lines
342. Tidewater Battery
343. Tidewater Biologicals
344. Tidewater Chemical
345. Tidewater Community College Chesapeake Campus
346. Tidewater Construction
347. Tidewater Dispose-All
348. Tidewater Drapery & Carpet Company
349. Tidewater Equipment
350. Tidewater Fibre
351. Tidewater Insulation
352. Tidewater Landscaping
353. Tidewater Mack
354. Tidewater Sand
355. Tidewater Septic Tank
356. Tidewater Spraying
357. Todd Co., Inc.
358. To BAK, Ltd.
359. Townsend Fuel, Inc.
360. Triangle Brick
361. Tri-City Hydraulic
362. Truckers' Rest Truck Stop
363. Twin B. Auto & Shopping Center
364. U-Haul of Tidewater
365. Ugine Industries

366. Union Oil Co. of Calif.
367. Vann, William, Truck
368. Vermont American International
369. Vico Construction Company
370. Vicon Farm Machinery Inc.
371. Village & V & Appliances
372. Village Square
373. Virginia Air Cond.
374. Virginia Beach Lot Clearing
375. Virginia-Carolina Tire
376. Virginia Door
377. Virginia Electric & Power Company
378. Virginia Engine Ltd.
379. Virginia Federal Savings & Loan
380. Virginia Graphic Systems
381. Virginia Precast
382. Virginie Tractor Co.
383. Volvo of America Corp.
384. Volvo Penta of America
385. WCPK Radio Station
386. Warehouse Equities
387. Warwick Manufacturing Company
388. Water Care of Tidewater
389. Waters Electric Corporation
390. Weaver Fertilizer
391. Wentz Hardware Supply
392. Wentz Marine Supply

393. Weyer Lacuser Company
394. White Farm Supply
395. White's Nursery
396. Whitehurst Paving
397. Whit Williams Inc.
398. Whitlow, Betterton & Co.
399. Whitlow, Smith Company
400. Williams Crane & Rigging
401. William Vann Trucking Company
402. Wilton, Ltd.
403. Wilson, The J. G., Corp.
404. Yellow Freight System, Inc.
405. Yellow River Ltd.

Staying Here

The Virginian-Pilot, Tuesday, August 5, 1980

Editor, Virginian-Pilot:

P. Hunter Cox of Chesapeake's industrial development agency was aggressive in providing industrial sites to national and/or international corporations.

Chesapeake has often been referred to as the "growth corridor of Tidewater." Since room for expansion in Norfolk is limited, isn't it better that these firms relocate to our sister city of Chesapeake than relocate out of Tidewater entirely? What's good for Chesapeake is good for Virginia Beach, Portsmouth, and Norfolk.

My congratulations to Mr. Cox. Perhaps Norfolk's industry hunters can learn from this experience.

W. B. MEREDITH II.

Norfolk.

Below are some of the prominent companies that moved to Chesapeake, VA:

BARNUM-BRUNS IRON WORKS, INC.

stment $12,000   No new employees

firm is located at 3052 Yadkin Road and is constructing
lding to store their finished doors.

VIRGINIA ELECTRIC & POWER COMPANY

vestment $760,600   *130 new employees*

ocated one mile south of Great Bridge on Battlefield oulevard, this new service/office building will be the eadquarters for the new district to serve 25,000 Chesaeake users of electricity and 3,300 users of natural s; construction to begin in October.

is facility should be singled out for particular credit

SWANN CHESAPEAKE TERMINAL CORPORATION

Investment $150,000 *No new employees*

ocated at 2801 South Military Highway, this fuel oil istribution center has expanded its facilities to include n office and a two-bay garage for maintenance and repair f its trucks. A radio tower has also been constructed for ontacting its trucks, as well as barges and tugs.

Foster Grant is the nation's leading maker of sunglasses. The plant also produces polymers, the basic materials used in the production of plastics. The $15 million plant was built in Chesapeake, VA on a 50-acre site on the Bank of The Southern Branch of the Elizabeth Pines in 1974.

FOSTER GRANT CO., INC.

vestment $3,800,000   20 new employee

:ated at 5100 Bainbridge Boulevard, this plastic nufacturing firm is expanding its operations by con ucting new buildings and acquiring new equipme provide additional high impact polystyrene capacity

Chesapeake's Industrial Transformation

From 1963 to 1970, Chesapeake relied heavily on the regional Tidewater Development Council to attract industry. However, much of the city's potential industrial land remained undeveloped. That changed in 1960 when former City Manager Robert House, Jr. emphasized the critical need for industrialization to broaden the tax base and create a balanced city.

In August 1970, under House's leadership, the Chesapeake Industrial Development Authority was established, and P. Hunter Cox was appointed as its director. House referred to Cox as "Super Salesman Cox," a fitting nickname for the energetic and results-driven leader. Cox, a pragmatic "doer" with little patience for bureaucratic red tape, quickly became a local legend, routinely presenting new industrial commitments to the city council on a monthly or bi-monthly basis.

Since mid-1970, Chesapeake announced over $75 million in new facilities and plant expansions. Cox proudly noted that Chesapeake, long regarded as a "bedroom community," had transformed into a city with a balanced 50-50 residential and industrial tax base.

The city is also anticipating federal funding to construct a cargo airport in Southern Deep Creek, while a new air facility near the Dismal Swamp is expected to spark development along a rural industrial parkway on US-17.

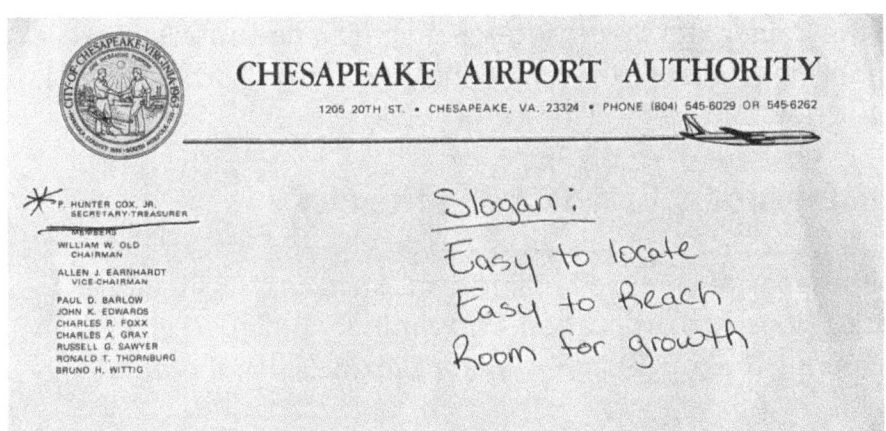

Airport letterhead 1975

Magazines like *Forbes* have recognized the South as the "new frontier" for economic growth, and Chesapeake continues to promote itself as the "City of the Future." Cox pledged to provide unwavering support to any desirable industry, large or small, considering Chesapeake as its future home.

Celebrating Industrial Growth and Community Support

Each year brings new challenges in the field of industrial development. While the arrival of new industries often collect attention, the expansion of existing facilities is just as significant, reflecting strong business growth.

The Chesapeake Industrial Development Department takes pride in both types of achievements. Cox expressed gratitude for the continued support of the Chesapeake City Council, city officials, civic organizations, and especially the citizens of Chesapeake. As the nation celebrated its bicentennial in 1976, Cox reflected on the principles that made the United States great and extended his best wishes for a bright future.

A Dream Realized: Expanded Channels and Infrastructure
Report by Hunter Cox

Hunter Cox was proud to report that all obstacles had been cleared for the 1.5-mile expansion of the 35-foot channel in the Southern Branch of the Elizabeth River. This development would make acres of prime industrial property available and enable existing industries to expand their import and export operations—a long-awaited dream come true.

Another significant project nearing completion was the half-mile section of I-464 in South Norfolk, including the Poindexter Street interchange. The new interstate would run parallel to Bainbridge Boulevard, connecting downtown Norfolk to I-64, improving industrial traffic flow across the Tidewater region.

"Industry, not a dirty word in the city"

Under Cox's leadership, Chesapeake attracted major firms such as Cargill, Inc., Noland Company, American Hoechst Corporation, and National Bulk Carriers. Many of these companies rank among the top 20 in *Fortune* magazine's list of the 500 largest firms.

Cargill, the world's largest independently owned grain company, and National Bulk Carriers, owned by billionaire Daniel K. Ludwig, are among the city's industrial giants. Cox attributed Chesapeake's success to a pro-industry city council that consistently supported growth.

"We're fortunate to live in a city that understands and supports industry," said Cox. He also acknowledged his 25 years of experience in industrial development as a key factor in attracting top-tier companies.

Shopping Centers on the Rise

Retail development was also booming in Chesapeake:

- The DeBartolo Corporation announced plans for a $33 million, 100-store regional shopping mall.

- The $30 million, 560,000-square-foot Greenbrier Mall opened in October 1981.

- Additional projects included the $7.5 million Branch Plaza Shopping Arcade near the new $2.7 million Hadges Ferry Bridge in Western Branch. The center featured 44 specialty shops, a supermarket, and a drugstore in a 150,000-square-foot space.

Standing Firm Against Unwanted Development

In 1981, Cox suspected a corporation linked to organized crime was attempting to buy waterfront property in South Norfolk. The corporation, owned by Stuart and Clifford Perlman of Caesar's World, Inc., operated casinos in Las Vegas, Lake Tahoe, and Atlantic City, NJ.

Cox was adamant: "We do not want the Perlman industries here. We will not show them land or sell them land in Chesapeake." Despite opposition, Cox stood firm, and the deal never materialized, protecting Chesapeake's reputation and future development.

A Visionary Leader

With Hunter Cox at the helm, Chesapeake transitioned from a quiet residential area to a thriving industrial and commercial hub. His bold strategies, unwavering determination, and commitment to ethical development set the foundation for the city's continued success as a beacon for industry on the East Coast.

'We have a city that wants industry, and willing to do what's necessary'

INDUSTRIAL DEVELOPMENT DEPARTMENT

1205 20th Street

Chesapeake, Virginia 23324

Telephone: (804) 545-6029 or 545-6262

P.H. Cox, Jr., Director

P. H. Cox, Jr.
Director

March 1976, Hunter at a Chesapeake City Council meeting.

Chapter 10:
Our Trip to Europe
- London, England
- Paris, France
- Vienna, Austria
- Steyr, Austria
- Athens, Greece

In 1971, while Hunter served as the Director of Industrial Development for the City of Chesapeake, we embarked on a trip to Europe to promote Virginia and encourage European industries to establish plants in Chesapeake, VA, USA. Our efforts were successful, and several businesses decided to invest in the region.

Our journey began in London, continued to Paris, and concluded in Austria. Below was our itinerary:

European Trip – February 2001

Our first trip to Europe, sponsored by Jim and Janice Hagenbuch, began on January 31, 2001. We departed Newark International Airport at 9:25 PM aboard a Boeing 747 and arrived at Heathrow Airport in England at 9:05 AM the following day.

- **February 2**: We visited the Swinderby International Antique Fair in Gresham.
- **February 3**: We toured Skipton Castle.
- **February 4**: Hunter and I departed for York.
- **February 5**: We attended the Newark International Fair, featuring 3,000 dealers.
- **February 6**: We stayed at the White House Regent Hotel in London.
- **February 7**: We visited the "White Cliffs of Dover"

White Cliffs of Dover

Hunter and his wife, Barbara in front of a button shop in Gresham

- **February 8**: Hunter and I visited "The Secret War Time Tunnels" in Dover, England at the White Cliff of Dover.

Secret War-Time Tunnels

Hotel at White Cliffs of Dover

Hunter's wife, Barbara in front of hotel

- **February 9**: We explored a London Underground station, I conducted research at the Metropolitan Archives, and then we embarked on a two-hour trip to Paris.

- **February 10**: We rode the Paris Metro.

- **February 11**: We visited a French flea market.

- **February 12**: We returned to Heathrow Airport and boarded a Boeing 747 for our flight back to the United States.

London, England

Gresham Family

<u>Sir Thomas Gresham</u>

Hunter's grandmother was Mary Edna Gresham. Her ancestry has been traced back to Sir Thomas Gresham of London, England, who was the son of Sir Richard Gresham. Sir Richard was the illustrious founder of the Royal Exchange and the Lord Mayor of London in 1537. The Gresham's immigrated to America in 1641. When Hunter and I went to London, we went to the National Portrait Gallery where there's a portrait of Sir Thomas Gresham in his fisherman's cap. I bought a fisherman cap for Hunter and took a photo of him in front of the portrait of Sir Thomas Gresham with his fisherman caps on too. It was a grand and glorious experience although I almost got arrested for taking a picture inside the building.

Sir Thomas Gresham

Sir Thomas Gresham, 1544
Reprinted with the kind permission of The Mercers' Company, London.

Tuesday, February 6th
London Metropolitan
Archives
+ Guild Hall Library
for research

Map of London

P.H. Cox, Jr., Director

Paris, France

Hunter and I traveled to Paris to see the world's famous Eiffel Tower.

Nord (train station) in Paris, France

Vienna, Austria

Vienna was the next city in Europe Hunter, and I visited to scout for new industries for Virginia, USA.

Map of Austria with Vienna circled

Flower of Austria (Edelweiss)

One company in particular, Plasser American Corporation built guns and gun shafts for Russia, but Hunter insisted they did the same for America by creating a plant in Chesapeake, VA. "If Russia has one- we need one in America also," said Hunter.

While Hunter and Bruno Kralowetz were visiting the Austrian gun plant and discussing business, I went shopping in the town of Steyr. I brought an Austrian suit, green in color, made of boiled wool and lining of red silk with small flowers. The lapels of the jacket had deer animal-like horns. Our last evening in Austria, we had dinner with Bruno Kralowetz and I wore the Austrian green suit I brought. As I made an entrance into the hotel dining room, Mr. Kralowetz bowed and kissed my hand then said, "Now you are an Austrian Lady." I smiled! Hunter and I had a wonderful trip, and the Austrians decided to build a plant in Chesapeake, VA, USA, named Plasser American Corporation. Mission accomplished!

Plasser American Corporation from Austria new plant in Chesapeake, VA

Gun Shaft created by Plasser American Corporation (American GFM Corporation)

april 25, 1979

Business

Machine-Tool Plant Opens in Chesapeake

By JOSEPH V. PHILLIPS
Virginian-Pilot Business Editor

American GFM Corp., a subsidiary of GFM Gesellschaft fur Fertigungstechnik und Maschinenbau Aktiengesellschaft, Steyr, Austria, dedicated a $9-million, 65,000-square-foot manufacturing plant Tuesday in Cavalier Industrial Park, Chesapeake. The plant will manufacture crankshaft milling machines, camshafts, and forging machines, mainly for suppliers of the American and Canadian automotive industry.

Virginia Gov. John N. Dalton, who spoke at the opening ceremony, said he anticipates an even greater investment in Chesapeake as GFM's business expands. "The manufacturing facility and offices completed so far are only a beginning," said Dr. Bruno Kralowetz, board chairman of both the American subsidiary and its Austrian parent. "Everything is planned and prepared in such a way that a future expansion to twice or four times the size is possible."

He said the company currently employs 31 people and hopes to double that figure this year and possibly increase it to more than 100 during 1980.

Dalton and Kralowetz paid tribute to state industrial development officials and P. Hunter Cox Jr., executive secretary of the Chesapeake Industrial Development Authority, for helping the firm locate in Chesapeake. Chesapeake Mayor Marian Whitehurst said she has high hopes that American GFM will become No. 1 in the machine-tool industry in the United States.

While in Vienna, we stayed at the historic Hotel Sacher "Wien", a fascinating and beautiful hotel. In the hotel's lobby, there was a memorable display: a tablecloth on an elegant table, signed by Russian leader Nikita Khrushchev and American President John F. Kennedy, with the embroidery done by Anne Sacher.

To celebrate our victory, Hunter and I enjoyed lunch at the hotel, finishing with the famous Sacher Torte for dessert. It was absolutely delicious!

Hotel Inter-Continental in Vienna

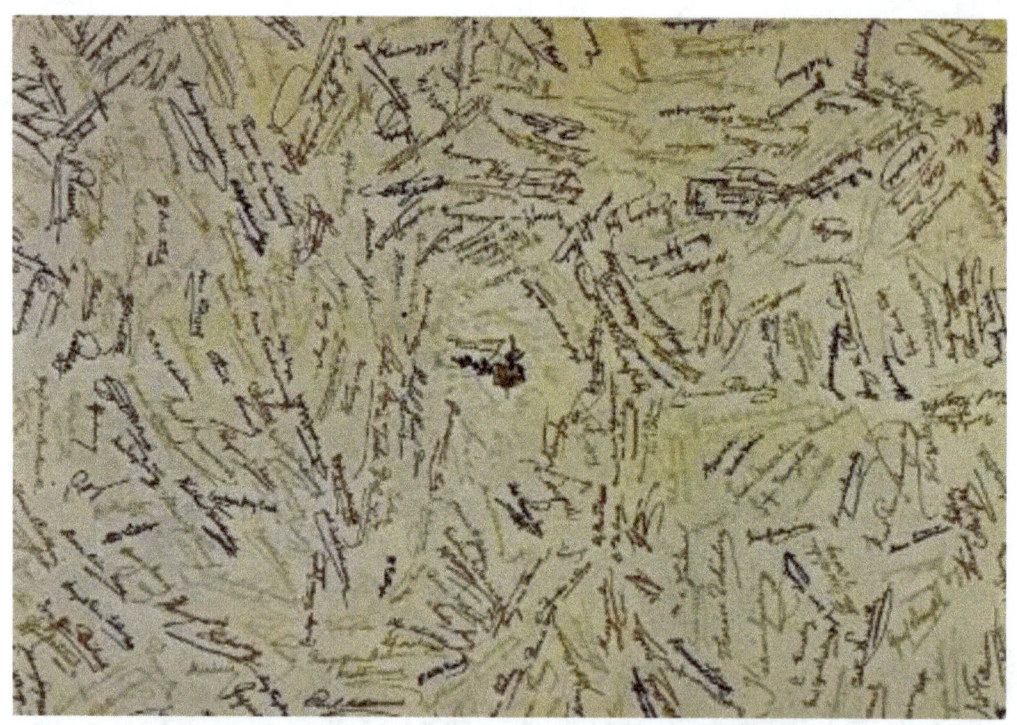
Elegant, embroidered tablecloth with signatures at Hotel Sacher "Wien"

The Cox embroidered tablecloth by Barbara Cox

Inspired by the experience, when we returned to America, I embroidered a Cox family tablecloth with our signatures. That tablecloth now resides in Suzanne's room.

The signatures were of:
Parke H. Cox, Sr
Davies Turner Cox
Paul C. Cox
Suzanne Cox
Parke Hunter Cox, III
Park Hunter Cox, Jr
Barbara Cox
Edward Sierra (Suzanne's husband at the time)

At the time of our trip, our son, Paul, had just graduated from Western Branch High School in Chesapeake, VA. Later, Paul was invited by Dr. Theo Mellick, the President of the Bank of Austria, and his wife to visit them in Vienna. He accepted the invitation and stayed for about a week, thoroughly enjoying the experience. It was his first and only trip to Europe, and it left a lasting impression on him.

P. Hunter Cox Jr.
. . . '$150 million industrial growth'

Steyr, Austria

Near the end of our trip, we went to Steyr, Austria, my favorite place. We stay at the "Hotel Minichmayr" where it is traditional to leave your shoes outside the door and to sleep on a feather bed. It was an enjoyable experience!

We went to the opera in Salzburg and went to the Grossglockner Mountains. Hunter rented a car one day and we drove to the Austrian Czechoslovakia borders. It was very exciting.

Hotel Minichmayr in Steyr, Austria

Athens, Greece

When Hunter and I went to Athens, Greece, we stayed at the Hotel at the foot of the Acropolis in the Parthenon. At night we saw the lights on the Acropolis as we went to sleep. It was beautiful! The Parthenon was built in 447BC and was twenty years in the building. It has been considered "the Architectural Glory of the World."

We went shopping in Athens and I bought two hand-crocheted vests and a lovely long, crocheted dress. We gave them to Sara and Anna, our granddaughters. They looked beautiful in them.

Chapter 11:
Volvo- The Mystery Company

Cox and the Volvo Corporation: A Chesapeake Legend

Cox's first interaction with the Volvo Corporation began through an intermediary—a consultant from The Fantus Company based in New Jersey. The consultant was initially vague, requesting information about 200-acre sites, the city, and port facilities, without revealing the identity of the client. However, Cox deduced that the client must be a manufacturing firm, given their interest in port facilities commonly used for importing and exporting goods.

The consultant returned, this time asking about 250-acre sites and seeking general information on traffic patterns and Interstate highway locations. When a third visit brought requests for 350-acre sites with Interstate access, rail facilities, topographic maps, and utility data, Cox's suspicions deepened. He became especially intrigued when the consultant asked about the height of railroad overpasses—information critical for transporting automobiles by train.

A conversation with a longshoreman friend at the port added another piece to the puzzle. The longshoreman mentioned a foreign individual inquiring about bringing auto parts into the country. Cox began gathering intelligence from his contacts at Ford Motor Company and learned that the foreign visitor was Swedish. With this detail, Cox connected the dots: the client was Volvo.

Determined to take the initiative, Cox bypassed the consultant and reached out directly to Björn Ahlström, President of Volvo of America. During their meeting, Cox expressed gratitude for Volvo's interest in Chesapeake, but Ahlström still refused to confirm any plans. Meanwhile, Cox continued working with The Fantus Company, showing them two competitive sites: the Cavalier Boulevard industrial area and the Greenbrier area.

As the consultant's requests grew to 500-acre sites, Cox, frustrated by the secrecy, decided to gamble on a bold move. He leaked a story to the local *Daily Press*, declaring that he wouldn't give Volvo a "free hunting license" on the land. "You don't get away with insulting and pushing a client into action too often," Cox later said, but this time, the gamble paid off. The leak acted as a catalyst, prompting Volvo to publicly acknowledge their interest. The company placed both sites under 30-day options at $30,000 per month each.

The rest, as they say, is history. Volvo ultimately chose the Greenbrier site, catapulting Chesapeake into international headlines. Volvo became the first foreign automobile manufacturer to assemble cars in the United States, a groundbreaking milestone in the auto industry.

On Tuesday, July 2, a groundbreaking ceremony for the $100 million Volvo plant was held at Greenbrier. Attendees included Virginia Governor Mills E. Godwin and Björn Ahlström. For Chesapeake, once merely known as a point 12 miles south of Norfolk, this achievement marked a significant step in industrial development.

To this day, the Volvo story is celebrated as a testament to the city's potential and promise. As Chesapeakians like to say, it was only the beginning of what Chesapeake would one day become. The Volvo story truly became a legend!

August 1, 1984

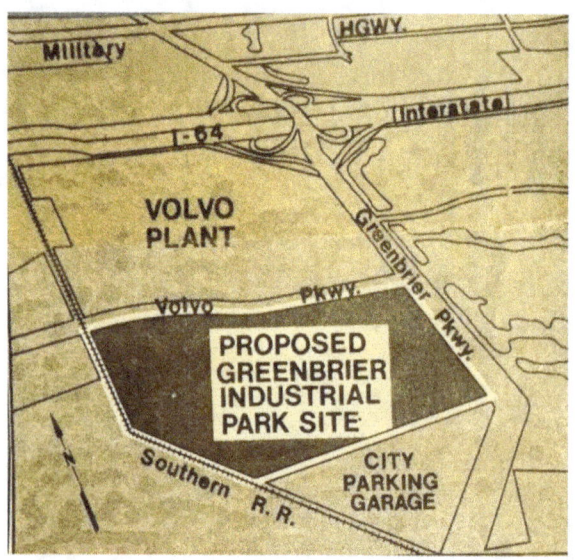

Volvo location in Greenbrier

VOLVO PENTA OF AMERICA, INC.

Value $700,000   50 Employees

Located at 816 Industrial Avenue, this firm is a subsidiary of Volvo of America Corporation and is one of the world's leading marine engine manufacturers. A Swedish company, this operation will market, sell, distribute and service their marine and industrial engines for the American market and for export.

GREENBRIER VOLVO, INC.

Value $1,000,000   30 Employees

Located at the southwest corner of South Military Highway and Greenbrier Parkway, this is a new car dealership for the Volvo automobiles.

Bjorn Ahlstrom ...
... U.S. Volvo Chief

'We are on target,' says Ahlstrom, spiking rumors that the Swedish automobile maker might abandon the Chesapeake project in the face of declining auto sales.

President of Volvo Company

Staff photo by Mike Williams

"IT'S GOING TO BE LIKE THIS"—Thomas McGinley, left, manager of the $1 million Greenbrier Volvo dealership to be built in Chesapeake, explains feature of the layout to Hunter Cox, center, head of industrial development for the City of Chesapeake, and Councilman Robert R. Carter at groundbreaking ceremony Wednesday. Work will start on construction in a few days and the facility is to be ready in November. The dealership is described as a "model retail transportation center."

april 27, 1989

John Harlow, president of Norfolk Truck Center, Inc., with one of the medium-duty trucks that Volvo sells in the United States

B9a Virginian-Pilot, Thursday, May 2, 1974

Sales and service operations will be separately housed at Volvo Greenbrier.

Ground Rites for Volvo Dealer

By LEON M. LARSON
Virginian-Pilot Business Editor

CHESAPEAKE—Officials of Volvo of America Corp. and a key sales subsidiary Wednesday ... that is expected to have an important role in upgrading the Swedish auto maker's U.S. franchise network.

The dealership, which will isolate sales and service in two separate buildings, will be built at S. Military Highway and Greenbrier Parkway, near the site of Volvo's planned $100-million-plus assembly plant.

Site clearing is expected to begin by May 15, and the dealership is scheduled to open in November, according to Cy Shelton, president of Volvo Capitol, Inc., a company-owned distributorship for nine Eastern and Southeastern states.

The dealership will operate as a subsidiary of Volvo Capitol, headquartered in Columbia, Md., but is designed to serve the entire U.S. dealer network, Shelton said.

Wednesday's ceremonies came as a prelude to the groundbreaking for the assembly plant itself, now scheduled for June, according to Charles P. Reed, general manager of Volvo's U.S. car marketing division.

The plant, the first to be announced by a foreign auto maker in this country, is scheduled to begin production in late 1976.

Reed said the dealership will become a major factor in providing improved "product support" for present and future Volvo buyers.

Ability to obtain such support or service may become the "predominant factor" in U.S. car marketing in the decade ahead, particularly in the price-quality level Volvo is dealing in, Reed said.

In establishing the model dealership the company will "start with the best thing we can conceive and go forward from there," the marketing executive continued.

Sales and service operations will be housed in separate buildings, repairs will be handled by teams of mechanics, and customers desiring to buy parts preparatory to doing their own repair work will be able to shop in a special full-display section, Volvo officials said.

Thomas P. McGinley, who will be general manager of the dealership, described the isolation of sales from repair and parts services as an "innovation in import car marketing" in the United States.

Volvo was scheduled to begin production in late 1976. Cox said, "We captured the $25 million Volvo plant for Chesapeake, VA. "We couldn't have paid for the publicity that plant brought us." Volkswagen Auto Company also had their eye on Chesapeake, but they were sidetracked by Volvo.

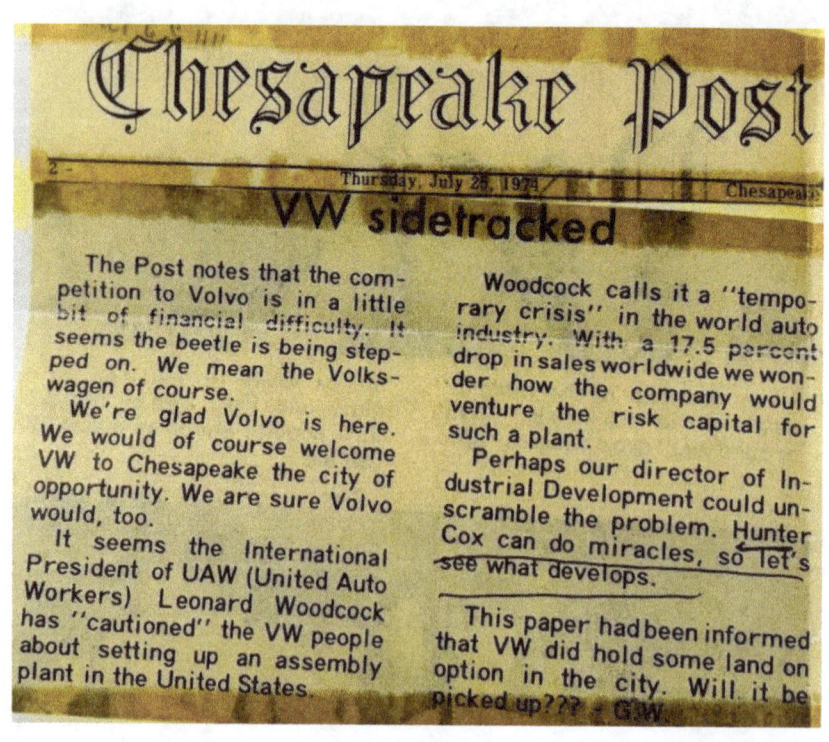

Chapter 12:
Hunter's Retirement

Hunter retired from Chesapeake around 1983, but our adventures were not over!

July 26, 1994

Hunter and I used to go to the **Eastern Shore Auction,** the chicken house for auctions. The place was called Barnyard Auctions, run by Otto W. Mears and his wife Violet.

Hunter at Bottle Show

Hunter's favorite handkerchief

Hunter and his wife, Barbara "Bobbie"

Hunter loading books into his van "a sticker van bulletin board on wheels"

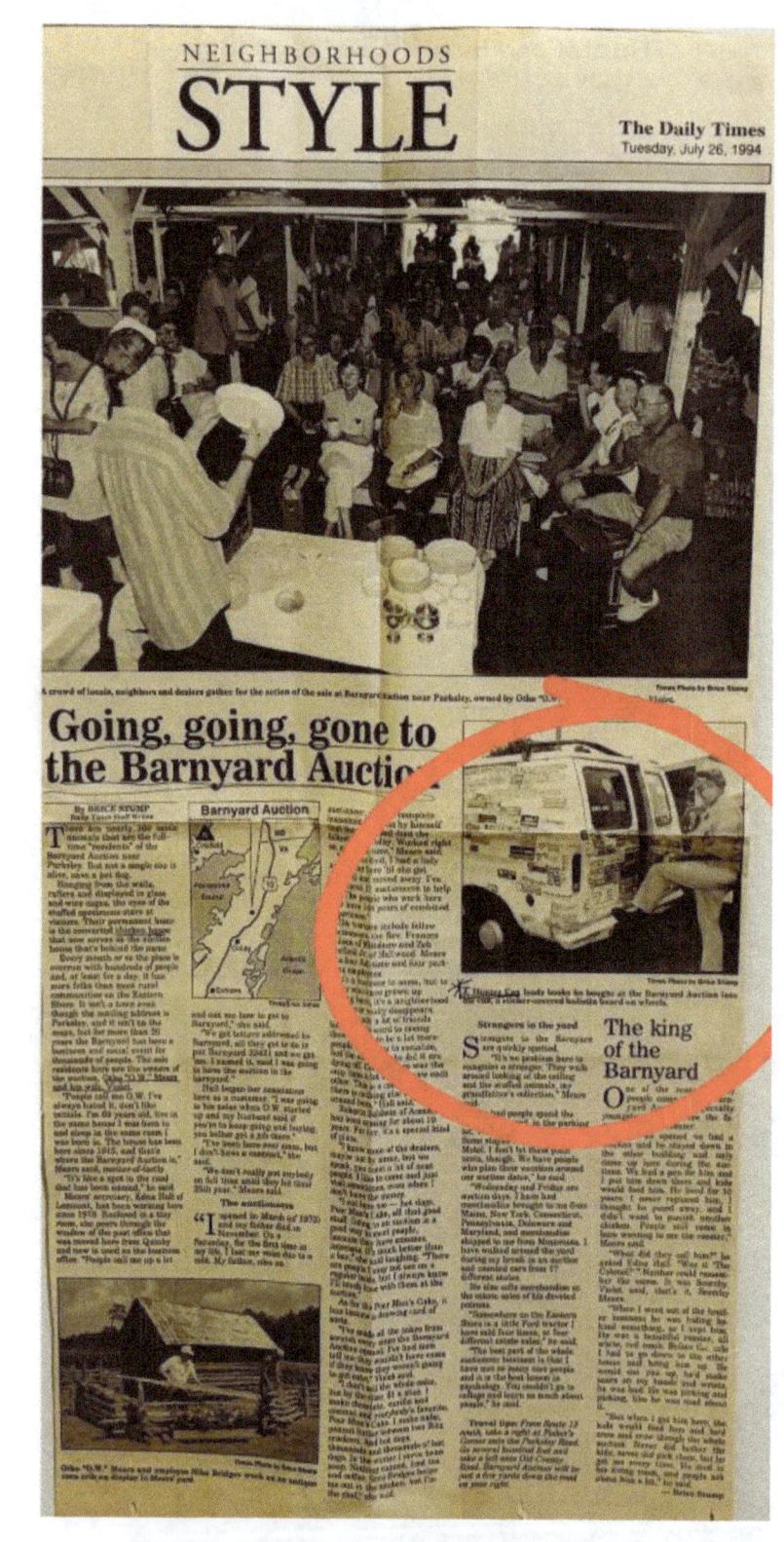

Hunter's "Sticker Van" made the paper

Amelung Tumbler

Adventures with Hunter Cox – Winter 1983
The Amelung Tumbler

Hunter Cox received a special request from Skinner's Auction House in Boston, one of his favorite places to visit for rare and valuable finds. The auction house, equally fond of Hunter, asked for his help in retrieving a remarkable piece of glass known as **The Amelung Tumbler**.

The tumbler had been discovered by the owner of an old antique hotel in Spring City, New Jersey, at a churchyard sale for just $50. Believing it to be of significant value, the owner wanted to consign it to Skinner's for auction. Naturally, Hunter agreed to help.

So, off we went—Hunter and I—in our "sticker van," embarking on an unforgettable winter adventure. It was cold and snowing when we left Chesapeake, Virginia, heading toward Spring City.

After a long drive, we arrived in Spring City and spent the night at a local hotel. Hunter assured me that traveling in an old, beat-up van was the perfect disguise—no one would suspect we were carrying anything valuable. He securely locked the Amelung Tumbler in the van before we turned in for the night.

The next morning, we began the journey to Boston. The snow was coming down hard by the time we reached Skinner's Auction House. Hunter, ever the careful guardian of fragile treasures, insisted I stay in the van. He was concerned that moving the tumbler from the cold van directly into the warm building might cause the glass to crack or shatter. "I'd probably cry if that happened," he confessed. I wholeheartedly agreed that I would cry too!

When Hunter unwrapped the tumbler inside, it was in perfect condition. Mission accomplished!

Skinner's Auction House later sold the Amelung Tumbler for a staggering $100,000,000. Today, this rare piece resides in the Metropolitan Museum of Art in New York City.

The Amelung Legacy
Country Magazine, 1980

John Frederick Amelung arrived in America with a group of skilled craftsmen, intending to establish a glass factory. Influenced by notable figures such as Charles Carroll of Carrollton, who owned land near Sugarloaf Mountain, Amelung chose the Sugarloaf site for his enterprise.

Recent research by the Corning Museum and the Smithsonian Institution has revealed that Amelung likely acquired an earlier glasswork, known as Foltz's Glass House, to serve as the foundation for his factory, which became known as **The Sugarloaf Mountain Glassworks**.

Despite producing exquisite, engraved pieces, the Amelung factory failed in 1795, leaving John Amelung destitute. He moved to Baltimore to live with his daughter and passed away in 1798 at the age of 57, never witnessing the acclaim his glassware would later achieve. To this day, the location of his grave remains unknown.

The engraved works of The Amelung Factory are now displayed at prestigious institutions, including the Smithsonian Institution in Washington, DC; the Corning Museum of Glass in Corning, New York; the Toledo Museum of Art in Ohio; and the Winterthur Museum near Wilmington, Delaware. The Metropolitan Museum of Art in New York proudly holds the famous engraved "Bremen" goblet, identified in 1928, alongside three rare tumblers from Amelung's factory.

It is believed that Amelung employed up to 400 craftsmen during the factory's decade-long operation, leading experts to speculate that more pieces of Amelung glass remain undiscovered.

The Amelung Tumbler engraved with "Bremen," now housed at the Metropolitan Museum of Art, is the very same tumbler that Hunter and I picked up from Spring City, NJ, and safely delivered to Skinner's Auction House.

What a journey it was!

*Chapter 13:
Sara's Interview*

Interview with Granddaddy
By Sara Cox

November 1, 2016

1. **Question:** What do you remember about your grandparents?

Answer: They were always Hardworking people who had my best interests at heart.

2. **Question:** Who were they?

Answer: Paul C. Cox & Maude Cox

3. **Question:** Where were they Born?

Answer: Paul: Sussex County Virginia; Maude: Petersburg, Virginia

4. **Question:** Where did they live when you knew them?

Answer: Surry, Virginia

5. **Question:** Did you see them often?

Answer: Yes

6. **Question:** What did you do with them?

Answer: I played cards with grandaddy and rode in his truck. My grandmother made peanut candy for me.

7. **Question:** What's your favorite food your grandmama made for you?

Answer: Peanut candy

8. **Question:** What was their job?

Answer: Paul - Business man: Ford automobile company, Surry; Maude - homemaker, Surry

9. **Question:** What kind of person were they?

Answer: Good people; I loved them very much

10. **Question:** How many kids did they have?

Answer: 3; Parke "Buster"; Roger; and Bernice

11. **Question:** How long has our family been in Surry?

Answer: 98 years

12. **Question:** Who was the first in our family to come over?

Answer: William Cox in 1630

13. **Question:** Do you have any stories about them? Can you share one?

Answer: Jes tons! Stories Below:

Paul Clifford Cox, my grandfather, lost a great deal of things when he encountered three fires. Before he got married, he lived in a rented home in Sussex. There he lost a lot of stuff in the house during the fire. After he got married, he lost everything in another fire. After he moved to Surry, he suffered through another fire involving his Business: Surry Ford Automobile.

14. **Question:** Do you have a favorite family English recipe?

Answer: Yes, Yorkshire Puddy

Sara and her sister, Anna

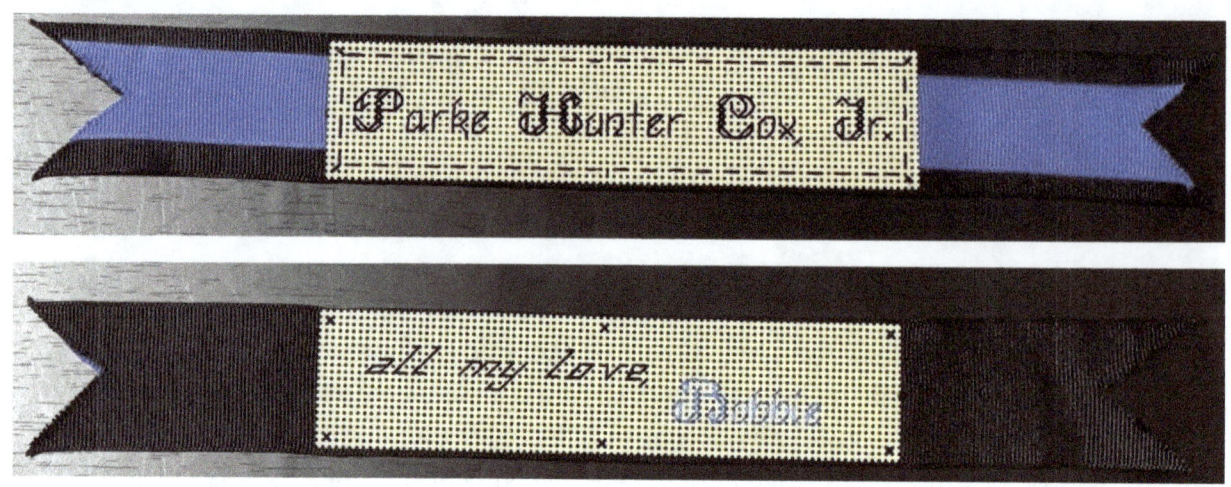

Bookmark made by Barbara "Bobbie"

Sara, Hunter's granddaughter

Pedigree Chart

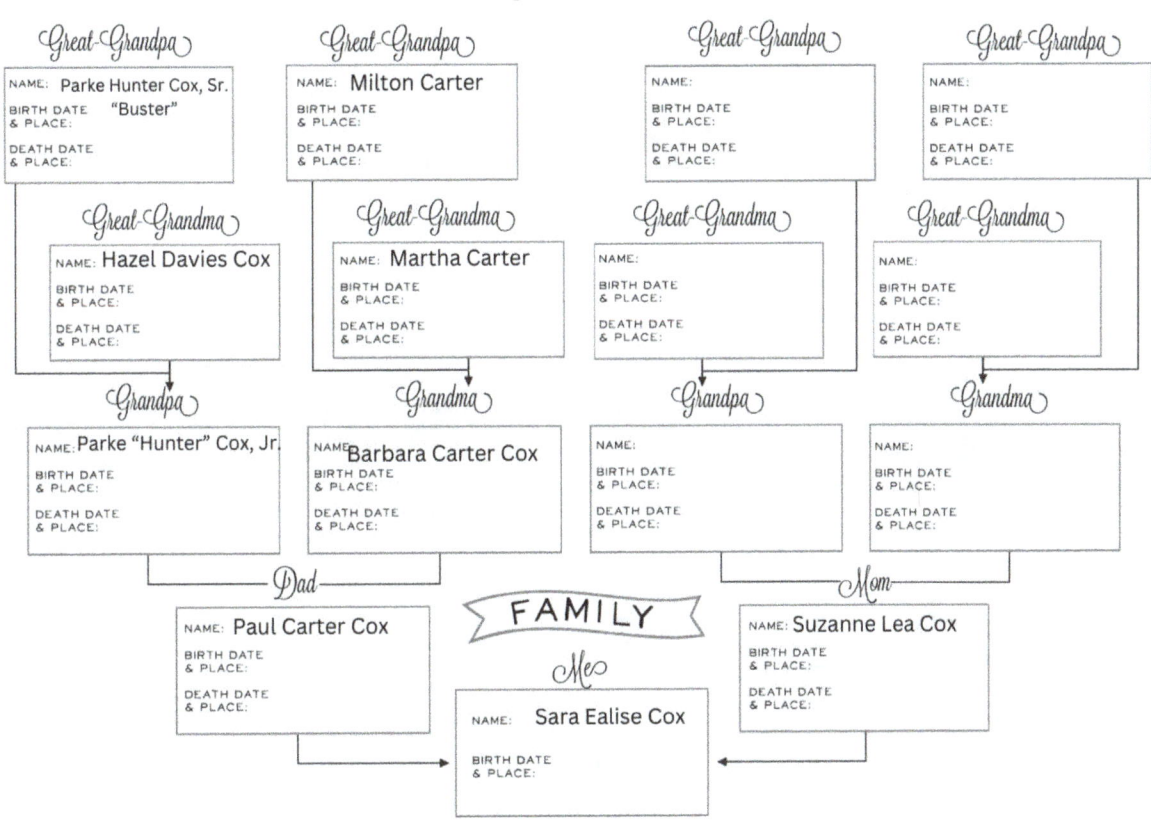

Chapter 14:
Hunter's Legacy

Obituary

Funeral Order of Service

Let us pray:

Our Father which art in heaven, hallowed be thy name.

Thy Kingdom come, thy will be done on earth, as it is in heaven.

Give us this day our daily bread.

And forgive us our debts, as we forgive our debtors.

And lead us not into temptation but deliver us from evil: For thine is the Kingdom, and the power, and the glory, forever. Amen.

This is the celebration of the life of a wonderful man, Parke Hunter Cox Jr.

Reading of the Obituary:

Parke Hunter Cox, Jr. passed away on February 20, 2022, at the age of 85. He was born in Surry, Virginia, on May 7, 1936, to Parke Hunter Cox and Hazel Davies Turner Cox. He was the grandson of Paul Clifford Cox and Maude Evelyn Cox.

Hunter attended the Augusta Military Academy and Hampden-Sydney College, where he excelled in basketball, baseball, and football. After graduating in 1957, he began his career with the Norfolk Redevelopment and Housing Authority. In just ten years, he advanced to become the administrative aide to the director of development. His next role was as the second-in-command at the Tidewater Virginia Development Council (TVDC) under Mayor Fred Duckworth. Robert House, the city manager of Norfolk at the time, said, "In his opinion, Hunter Cox was the most successful industrial development man he had the experience of working with."

In 1971, Hunter became the Director of Industrial Development for the City of Chesapeake. From his small office in South Norfolk, he helped secure over $165 million in industrial investments, attracted 38 new and expanding industries, and created 783 job opportunities. Hunter played a key role in the development of Greenbrier Mall, the first regional shopping center in the city, which opened in 1981.

He also spearheaded the construction of Chesapeake Municipal Airport, a general aviation cargo airport for private aircraft.

Under Hunter's leadership, 42 industries were located in Chesapeake between 1973 and 1974, including Foster Grant, Plasser American Corporation, and Volvo. Foster Grant, a sunglasses manufacturer, and Plasser American, an Austrian company that produced railroad maintenance equipment, were notable companies that thrived in the area. Volvo also established its first U.S. manufacturing operation in Chesapeake's Greenbrier Industrial area, investing $150 million in an auto assembly plant that employed 3,500 people. Volvo produced innovative transit buses at this plant, including the iconic articulated buses designed to navigate tight city streets. Hunter earned the nickname "Smooth-Talking Industrial Hunter" and became a legendary figure in industrial development.

Hunter is survived by his wife, Barbara Ann Carter Cox, and their three children: Parke Hunter Cox III and his wife, Lisa Ann Bowker Cox; Suzanne Cox Stickle and her husband, Joseph Walter Stickle; and Paul Carter Cox and his wife, Suzanne Lea Schomberg Cox. He is also survived by six grandchildren: Jaclyn Martin Kowal and her husband, Nathan Peter Kowal; Carter Cox Martin and his wife, Katherine Kimiko Arita Martin; Parke Hunter Cox IV; Sarah Ealise Cox; and Anna Elizabeth Cox, along with a great-grandson, Camden Samuel Martin.

Committal:

Scripture- Psalm 23:

The Lord is my shepherd; I shall not want.

He maketh me to lie down in green pastures: he leadeth me beside the still waters.

He restoreth my soul: he leadeth me in the paths of righteousness for his name's sake.

Yea, though I walk through the valley of the shadow of death, I will fear no evil: for thou art with me; thy rod and thy staff they comfort me.

Thou preparest a table before me in the presence of my enemies: thou anointest my head with oil; my cup runneth over.

Surely goodness and mercy shall follow me all the days of my life: and I will dwell in the house of the Lord forever.

Benediction:

May the grace of the Lord Jesus Christ, and the love of God, and the communion of the Holy Spirit be with us all. Amen.

The Hunter Cox family received many heartfelt letters of sympathy and condolences from colleagues, neighbors, and friends. Among those who expressed their support were:

- Marty and Roger Lantz
- Norman Heckler and family
- Ed DeHaven
- Donald E. Taylor
- Jim and Janice Hagenbuch

From:

Grand Lodge A. F. & A. M. of Virginia

Masonic Temple

Parke Hunter Cox, Jr. was a member of Corinthian Lodge number 266 with the degree of fellowcraft and degree of Master Mason under the hand of the most Worshipful Grand Master of Masons in Virginia and of the seal of our Grand Lodge this first day of March Anno Lucis 5961 Anno Domini 1961.

The Most Worshipful
Grand Lodge of Ancient, Free and Accepted Masons
of the Commonwealth of Virginia

Edmund C. Haner Jr. Grand Master

To all whom these Presents may concern, Greetings:

Know ye, that the bearer hereof, our well beloved Brother PARKE HUNTER COX, JR. hath been regularly initiated into the mysteries of Ancient Freemasonry, passed to the Degree of **Fellowcraft** and raised to the sublime Degree of **Master Mason** in CORINTHIAN Lodge No. 266, A.F. & A.M. under our jurisdiction and that he hath been regularly examined in open Lodge on the work of each of these aforesaid degrees and having satisfied his brethern of his knowledge thereof, they have, by ballot, declared him proficient in the three catechisms.

Therefore, for his diligence and interest in Freemasonry, we have granted him this Diploma as a mark of our esteem, thereby recommending him to the attention and confidence of all Ancient, Free and Accepted Masons, who are good and true and to whom he may present himself. That this Diploma may not be used by anyone else we have caused our Brother to place his Common signature in the margin hereof.

Given under the hand of the Most Worshipful Grand Master of Masons in Virginia and of the seal of our Grand Lodge this 1st day of MARCH Anno Lucis 5961, Anno Domini 1961

Teste:

Archer B. Gay Grand Secretary

the Common signature of Parke Hunter Cox Jr.

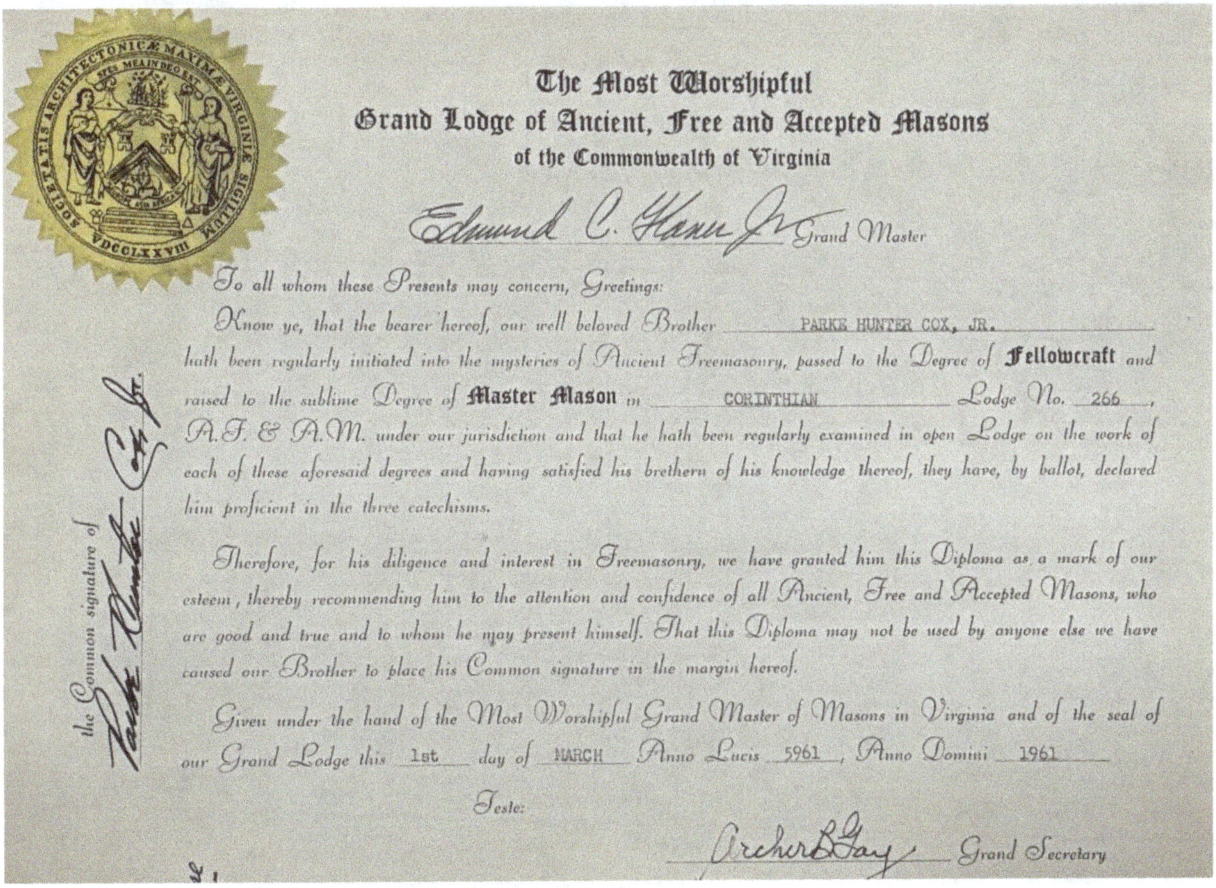

Mason Certificate

Monument at Blandford Cemetery in Petersburg, Virginia

February 23, 2022

I want to share a story that reflects my father's incredible capacity for unconditional love and forgiveness. Over the years, my dad, Hunter Cox, touched the lives of countless people across Virginia. In the past couple of weeks, my family and I have been deeply moved by the many heartfelt stories and memories shared with us. Today, I would like to share one of my own.

I remember a dark time in my life when I ignored my parents' wisdom and found myself facing the painful consequences. I experienced a loss I could never have imagined, and it left me with regret and shame. I felt trapped in the mess I had rushed into, unsure of how to move forward.

As I wrestled with what to do, I couldn't stop worrying about what my father would say. The last thing I wanted was to embarrass him. He was a good man—a loving father and a devoted husband to my mother. I didn't want others to think he and my mother hadn't raised me with strong values. But despite my hesitation, I knew I had no other option. I needed help rebuilding my life, and I knew I had to face my dad.

When I finally decided to return to my parents' home, I will never forget what I found. My dad was standing in the driveway, waiting for me, with his arms wide open. As I stepped out of the car, he wrapped me in a hug and simply said, "Welcome home."

There was no shame. No blame. No condemnation. Only love.

In that moment, my dad showed me a glimpse of God's unconditional love. Just as my father welcomed me, God welcomes us when we bring our sins, failures, brokenness, pain, and hurt to Him. He wraps us in His arms and says, "Welcome home." It reminded me of the story of the Prodigal Son in the Bible—a story of grace, redemption, and the healing power of God's love.

My father displayed that same grace to me, and I will carry the memory of his love with me forever. The same invitation is open to all of us. If you seek forgiveness and accept the love of Jesus Christ, my Lord and Savior, you too can experience that unconditional love.

With love,
Suzanne Cox Stickle

December 4, 2024

My Daddy

I love my daddy. He was the greatest dad and excelled in everything he did. His unique vision in real estate was truly remarkable. He took the time to study, understand, and weigh the advantages and disadvantages of each opportunity, and he was exceptional at it.

Daddy and I walked many pieces of property in Surry, a place he loved deeply. He helped me purchase my first home and offered invaluable advice, like putting up a fence and installing a deep well—decisions that continue to pay dividends daily. His advice was always honest, truthful, and accurate. Those who listened to his wisdom reaped the benefits. It was a gift to know I could trust him implicitly, knowing he'd never mislead me.

He had a remarkable ability to turn negative situations into positive ones, and I loved him all the more for it. I miss his guidance deeply. My daddy let me be myself and stood by me, defending and supporting me. I cherish him for that. He was a good man and an incredible role model.

I'll never forget the time he carried me down the hall at Saint Paul's hospital after my asthma attack, never leaving my side. He even helped cure me of asthma.

Daddy was also a champion golfer, and I'll always treasure the memory of witnessing his hole-in-one at City Park. He excelled in everything he touched. Some of my favorite moments were watching baseball, football, and basketball games with him. He shared his love of sports, history, and preserving history with me, and I learned so much from him. He still had more to teach, but I am forever grateful for the lessons I did learn.

One of the most selfless acts I'll always remember is when he brought me a mattress all the way from North Carolina—even though he had the flu. He never complained, never uttered a grumble, even in discomfort.

I will never be able to thank him enough for the countless ways he guided and supported me throughout my life. But I know he understood how much I appreciated him. My love for him goes beyond words. He was perfect in my eyes, and I aspire to be just like him. I miss him more than words can express, but I look forward to seeing him again in heaven. I will forever love, honor, and miss him.

Love,
Paul

Dear Dr. Zahan,

I want to express my heartfelt gratitude for the exceptional care you provided to my father, Parke Hunter Cox, Jr. Your dedication to his well-being, your collaboration on his treatment, and your visits to our family meant the world to us.

Your care not only extended his life but also allowed him to enjoy it as much as possible. He often spoke of you with the highest regard, praising your expertise and compassion. He truly thought the world of you and your staff.

Words cannot fully capture the depth of our appreciation for your service. You will always hold a special place in our hearts.

With sincere gratitude,
Paul Cox

Conclusion:
A Life Well Lived

As we close the final chapter of Parke Hunter Cox Jr.'s remarkable story, we are reminded of the timeless truth that a life lived with love, faith, and purpose echoes far beyond its earthly bounds. Hunter's journey was one of devotion—to his family, his community, and the values that defined him. He gave generously, loved deeply, and inspired all who had the privilege of knowing him.

Through his faith in God, he found the strength to see the best in others and the courage to create a brighter future. His unwavering moral compass and disciplined approach to life set a standard that continues to guide those he left behind. As a husband, father, businessman, and friend, Hunter lived a life that reflected grace, humility, and a passion for making a difference.

Although Hunter is no longer with us, his legacy lives on in the lives he touched. His laughter, his wisdom, and his steadfast love remain etched in our memories, serving as a beacon of hope and inspiration. We honor him by carrying forward his lessons: to love without limits, to lead with integrity, and to always seek the greater good.

This book is not just a story—it's a celebration of a man whose life reminds us all to live with purpose and faith. Parke Hunter Cox Jr. will forever be a testament to the power of a life well lived. He is deeply missed, profoundly loved, and always remembered.

With gratitude and love,
Barbara (Bobbie)

Hunter and Barbara Cox

Acknowledgment

November 2024

Paul,

Thank you for giving me advice and encouragement for Hunter's book. You were such a productive person with many interests. I hope I have documented everything.

Love,

Mama

Paul Carter Cox, Hunter's son

www.ingramcontent.com/pod-product-compliance
Lightning Source LLC
Chambersburg PA
CBHW060410010526
44107CB00005B/639